HOBO QUILTS

Dear Jiji,
Merry Christmas;
may you keep & tell
your magic & secretz
in the sacred fabric
of your quilts!
♡A

2023

HOBO QUILTS

55+ Original Blocks
Based on the Secret Language
of Riding the Rails

Debra G. Henninger

Krause Publications
Cincinnati, Ohio

Hobo Quilts: 55+ Original Blocks Based on the Secret Language of Riding the Rails. Copyright © 2010 by Debra G. Henninger. Manufactured in China. All rights reserved. The patterns and drawings in this book are for the personal use of the reader. By permission of the author and publisher, they may be either hand-traced or photocopied to make single copies, but under no circumstances may they be resold or republished. No other part of this book may be reproduced in any form or by any electronic or mechanical means including information storage and retrieval systems without permission in writing from the publisher, except by a reviewer who may quote brief passages in a review. Published by Krause Publications, an imprint of F+W Media, Inc., 4700 East Galbraith Road, Cincinnati, Ohio, 45236. (800) 289-0963. First Edition.

14   13   12   11   10   5   4   3   2   1

www.fwmedia.com

DISTRIBUTED IN CANADA BY
FRASER DIRECT
100 Armstrong Avenue
Georgetown, ON, Canada L7G 5S4
Tel: (905) 877-4411

DISTRIBUTED IN THE U.K. AND EUROPE BY
DAVID & CHARLES
Brunel House, Newton Abbot, Devon, TQ12 4PU, England
Tel: (+44) 1626 323200, Fax: (+44) 1626 323319
E-mail: postmaster@davidandcharles.co.uk

DISTRIBUTED IN AUSTRALIA BY
CAPRICORN LINK
P.O. Box 704, S. Windsor NSW, 2756 Australia
Tel: (02) 4577-3555

Library of Congress Cataloging in Publication Data
Henninger, Debra G.
 Hobo quilts : 55+ original blocks based on the secret language of riding the rails / Debra G. Henninger.
    p. cm.
 Includes index.
 ISBN 978-1-4402-0412-8 (alk. paper)
 1. Patchwork--Patterns. 2. Quilting--Patterns. I. Title.
 TT835.H444 2010
 746.46'041--dc22

                                          2009048282

Editor: Jennifer Claydon
Designer: Michelle Thompson
Production Coordinator: Greg Nock
Photographer: Ric Deliantoni (unless otherwise noted)
Cover Stylist: Jan Nickum

METRIC CONVERSION		
TO CONVERT	**TO**	**MULTIPLY BY**
Inches	Centimeters	2.54
Centimeters	Inches	0.4
Feet	Centimeters	30.5
Centimeters	Feet	0.03
Yards	Meters	0.9
Meters	Yards	1.1

About the Author

Debra Henninger is an active member of the quilt community. She owns three quilt shops and attends national and regional quilt shows. Debra also operates and organizes quilt cruises and retreats. In addition to being a quilter, Debra is also a history and railroad enthusiast.

Dedication

This book is dedicated to my husband, Mark, and my children, KeriAnn, Julia and Gregory, who have always had to cope with my workaholic ways. I love you so much.

Acknowledgments

I am blessed to be surrounded by the most talented, creative, giving quilters one could ever hope to be associated with. Thank you, Sharon Janzen, for believing in the project and always being there to sew and edit. Thank you, Debby Greenway, for your creativity, hard work and dedication. Thank you, Robyn Welch, for your willingness to travel at a moment's notice and help with the research. Thank you, Jeri Rennie, for doing all you could and being my best friend. Additional thanks to the women who sewed, quilted and bound the projects so wonderfully: Claudette Cremer, Wendy Russell, Barb Sidell, Suz Tealby, Alice Braman, Sherrie Coppenbarger, Diana Snyder, Arvella Utley, Susie Smith, Kathi Lehman, Jan Mishler, Theresa Cobb, Georjean Lipovsky, Lilian Cagle, Connie Markley, Jeanette Hammond and Linda Ward.

CONTENTS

INTRODUCTION

When I was a child, my mom, Juanita Penman, would tell the story of her great-grandmother feeding the hobos. Her great-grandmother was an excellent cook, and the fence post was marked to let all hobos know they would be fed for doing chores.

My mom also taught my sister, Cindy, and me to sew as young girls. I carried those lessons with me and have owned and operated quilt shops for over 13 years. I am always on the hunt for new, fun, innovative ideas in the quilting world. These facts, combined with a love of family history and a degree in Sociology, made this book a natural for me.

Most people I talk to have a connection with hobo lore; whether their family fed the hobos, worked for the railroads, or were hobos. From the 1880s to the 1940s, hobos were a part of American life, with up to 250,000 travelers on the road at one time. Some viewed the hobos as dirty, hard-drinking, untrustworthy bums. Most saw them as honest, honorable people caught in extraordinary times. All would agree, however, that the railroads crisscrossing this country were the lifeblood of every hobo. Hobo signs were their secret language: They gave direction and advice to the savvy traveler including where to find food, water, a place to sleep and possibly work. Based on these signs, hobos could tell how they would be received by a home owner, the police, a community or even a dog. The meanings of hobo signs reflect all sides of the transient life, from the honorable to the unsavory. These signs also tell the story of what it took to survive as a hobo. Most importantly, this subculture was a significant part of American history that is worthy of remembrance.

HOW THIS BOOK WORKS

The blocks in this book are all 6" square when finished. Most are pieced, but some are appliquéed, and a few are paper pieced. Most of the blocks are simple and quite appropriate for beginners, but those blocks that have multiple small pieces are more appropriate for intermediate quilters. Fabric requirements for the blocks are omitted because these blocks are perfect for scraps and the fabric requirements will vary greatly depending on how many blocks you wish to make.

Fabrics

I tried to choose fabrics that reminded me of hobo clothing, such as plaids, stripes and homespun. Most of the fabric is from the Windham Basics line of fabrics because, as a shop owner, I know how frustrating it is to see a quilt made from a fabric line that is no longer available. I have been assured that Windham Basics will be available for a long time, so you will be able to replicate the look of the blocks in this book if you choose. However, if you want to add your own design flair to these blocks, there are many other suitable fabric lines.

Traditional Pieced Blocks

Because the blocks are small and have multiple seams, I strongly recommend using a scant ¼" seam whenever possible. The block patterns are laid out as a graphic of the block with the individual pattern pieces shown below it. The cutting size of each piece is written below the image of the piece. If the piece is a triangle, the size given is the square you will cut; cut this square diagonally to create the triangles.

Most of the blocks are simple enough to easily understand where the pattern pieces are to be placed. However, some of the blocks are complex. In these cases, I have labeled the pattern pieces. In either case you should lay the block out once you have all the pieces cut to make sure you have all the pieces needed and that the finished block will be correct.

If you are making the same block multiple times, production method is best. Repeating the same step in an assembly line will save you time and cut down on mistakes.

Appliquéd Blocks

The appliqué blocks in this book are very simple and great for beginners. I always begin these blocks with an 8" background square to compensate for shrinkage that will occur. When I'm completely done stitching around the appliqué, I then trim the block to 6½". This step ensures that the block is the correct size and also allows you to center your appliqué. To make these blocks, you will need to use a fusible web; I use Steam-a-Seam Lite, but you can use any product you prefer. Follow the manufacturer's instructions for your choice of fusible web. Here is the method I suggest for making the appliqué blocks:

1 Photocopy the appliqué pattern from the book, then trace the appliqué pattern on the back side of the photocopy. If you don't do this, your appliqué will be mirror imaged.

2 If there are pieces that bump up against each other, decide which one logically would sit behind the other. Extend the line of this piece so that it can be fused under the top piece.

3 Trace the individual pieces onto the paper side of the fusible web. Cut out the pieces outside the drawn lines, leaving extra fusible web around the shape.

4 Fuse the fusible web onto the wrong side of the fabric, then cut out the fused fabric shapes.

5 Peel the paper backing off of the fusible web and fuse the piece to the block's base fabric. If you use an appliqué pressing sheet (which I highly recommend) you can fuse the shapes directly to the appliqué sheet with the photocopied pattern below it and you will be able to achieve perfect placement.

6 To give the block a homespun, primitive look, stitch around the appliqué with a blanket stitch using a dark cotton thread.

Paper Pieced Blocks

The paper pieced blocks in this book are extremely easy. The pattern appears backwards compared to the finished block, and the pieces are numbered in the order you will be sewing. To start, you will need foundation paper; you can use photocopy paper, but a good quality foundation paper will make the job much easier. I use Carol Doak Foundation Paper. You will also need straight pins. I recommend flower pins because they lay flat. To make the paper easier to tear away, shorten your stitch length and use a #90 needle. However, don't tear the paper away until your project is finished. Here is a quick step-by-step guide to paper piecing the blocks in this book:

1 Photocopy the paper piecing pattern; make a copy for each block you plan to make. The pattern pieces are numbered in the order you will sew. Add a ¼" seam allowance line completely around the block pattern.

2 Place your fabric right side up on the back (nonprint) side of the piece marked 1 on

the paper. Make sure your fabric generously covers the area with at least ¼" of fabric beyond the pattern section. You can hold the pattern and fabric to the light to check. Pin this piece of fabric in place.

3 Place the fabric for pattern piece 2 right side down on top of the first fabric. You will be stitching both fabrics and the paper on the line between pattern pieces 1 and 2. Before you stitch, check that fabric 2 will generously cover pattern piece 2 once you have stitched and pressed fabric 2 to the right side.

4 Turn the paper pattern over with the print side up. Stitch on the line between pieces 1 and 2.

5 Trim the seam allowance of your seam to ¼" and finger press fabric 2 to the right side.

6 Continue to attach pieces in this manner, following the numbers on the pattern until the block is complete. Trim the block to 6½" square.

Hobo Sign Quilt Blocks

Paper piece

I was very curious as to whom these men could be and as soon as I saw Great Aunt Iva, I began bombarding her with questions. She explained that they were men riding in railroad cars around the country looking for work and they were called "hobos" and that it was very dangerous because railroad men called "bulls" tried to keep them off the trains in quite brutal means.

— JUANITA PENMAN,
Tennessee

2" × 4½" (2)   1½" × 4½" (3)   1½" × 6½" (2)

ANYTHING GOES

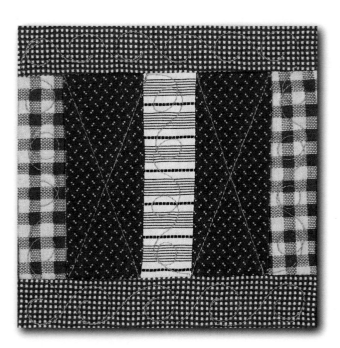

Another time in Colorado, I got into a boxcar at night, unaware that a dead man was also inside; learned this later when I accidently stumbled over him. This was a terrifying experience. I stood in the doorway for miles, trying to think what I must do. The train did finally slow enough and stopped to take on water. Immediately, I jumped out and ran as far and as fast as I could into a field. There I waited until the train pulled out. By that time it was beginning to be daylight. I helped a work crew sort bolts and nuts for two days for my meals. A train stopped the second day for water. I got on it and got off at Pueblo, Colorado, where I overheard someone saying that a fellow that was found on the train had been stabbed in Elko, Nevada.

— BILLY A. WATKINS,
Indiana

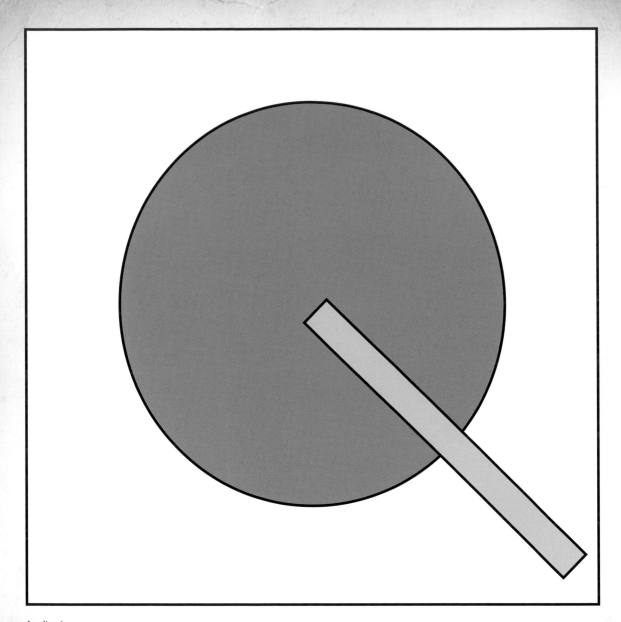

Appliqué

Another thing I remember, that on the main lines across the country when one train met one going the other way that there would be thirty to forty transits on each train, each going to where they hoped the work would be. They would yell back and forth asking where the work was.

— LYLE A. O'HARE,
Texas

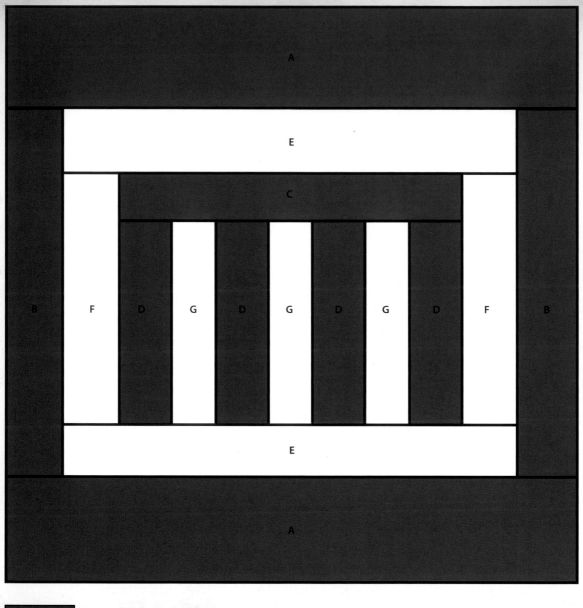

A
1¼" × 6½" (2)

B
1" × 5" (2)

C
1¼" × 4½"(1)

D
1⅛" × 2¾"(4)

E
1¼" × 5½" (2)

F
1" × 3½" (2)

G
1" × 2¾" (3)

I had met a fellow my age, who (I learned later) was an escaped convict from a prison in Iowa. We stayed together for a while, and he learned all about me and my family (mother and dad). He called them collect and asked them for money for me to pay him for caring for me. Mother wired $100, but I had to identify my grandma Pringle (Mother's maiden name) by her first name to get the money. I went to the telegraph office with this guy and when I found out what was needed for identification, I thought "Oh ____, I don't know her first name," and told the operator so. He said I couldn't get the money unless I did. That's when I really started trying to remember everything Mother had ever told me. Then I remembered that Mother had said one time that Aunt Mary was named after her mother. I hollered out "Mary." The guy smiled and gave me the money. I split from the convict. Moral: Always listen to your parents when they are telling you something.

— CHARLES R. DOTY,
Oklahoma

1¼" × 6½" (2)   1½" (2)   1⅞" (12)   1½" × ⅞" (1)   2" × 1½" (2)   1½" × 6½" (1)   1½" × ⅞" (2)   1⅞" (12)

22

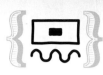

I am 70 years old now and left home when I was 14 and hitchhiked and rode the rails looking for work. That was back in the days when you worked for a dollar a day and room and board—if you could find work.

When harvest time came around, you could make $2.00 a day shocking grain or hauling bundles (of grain). Lots of times, your room to sleep in was on the ground under a bundle wagon or in the hay loft of the barn.

When you ran out of clean clothes, you got a bucket (pail) and some soap and water and either rubbed them on a scrub board or stomped them up and down in the pail with a stomper. When you got them as clean as you could, you twisted them to wring the water out and hung them on a fence or bush to dry.

Washing in cold water was an everyday occasion. You either pumped the water by hand from a well or got some from a farmer's stock tank or lake or river.

If you were going very far, you usually carried a bed roll that was an old blanket or two, and if you were lucky to have an extra pair of socks, pants and shirt, you rolled them up in the bed roll. When you were on a moving train in an empty boxcar, you used the bed roll to sit on so

(Continued on next page.)

you didn't get slivers in your butt from bouncing around on the wood floors. When the train pulled into a town and stopped, the railroad Bulls (cops) would walk the length of the train and try and kick all the hobos off. If we weren't ready to leave, we would close the doors and leave a couple of inches open so we could see out and they couldn't lock the doors on us. Before we got in the car, we would always pick up some small sticks to make wedges out of so we could stick them in between the door rollers and the car so nobody could slide the door shut or open it to see if someone was inside.

Eating was always a problem because trains don't stop for lunch. We used to get a couple cans of pork and beans and a loaf of bread (cost 25 cents or less). That would last 2 people a whole day.

Every town had what was called a Jungle. That was a hidden spot a ways away from the tracks where the hobos made camp. They could build a camp fire and boil some coffee or cook some vegetables while looking for work or waiting for another train. They used tin cans to cook in and eat and drink out of. Just about everybody carried a pair of pliers and a pocket knife. The old Boy Scout knife was a handy one to have because it had a bottle opener, screw driver and can opener besides a blade or two.

Most of the people you met were pretty open and friendly but there was always the few that you couldn't trust, and if you had any money, you didn't let anyone know about it.

When I was 18 years old, I was working on a farm at Kidder, South Dakota, and, in June, a friend and I decided to go to Kansas and follow the harvest back up to South Dakota. We left here with $10 between us and made it to Wichita, Kansas, in about a week. We rode the boxcars most of the way but had to do some hitchhiking too, and that wasn't worth a damn. There had been a few killings and robberies and nobody would give us a lift. One day, we walked close to 25 miles, and we got one ride for 3 miles. When we got there, it took a day or two to find a job, but we both got a job at the same place pitching bundles for $2.50 a day and room and board.

Nobody worked on Sundays in those days so when Saturday night came around, everybody went to town. We would draw a few dollars out of our wages and go along. The 'bos usually had to go to town anyhow to get supplies for the next week so we got a ride to town. We didn't have to be back till Monday morning so we would look for some bootleg whisky and wild women. We usually got back home by Sunday afternoon and had time to wash some clothes and get a good night's sleep before work on Monday.

— DEAN WEBB,
South Dakota

Photograph by Dorothea Lange, Courtesy of the Library of Congress, lc-usz62-55378

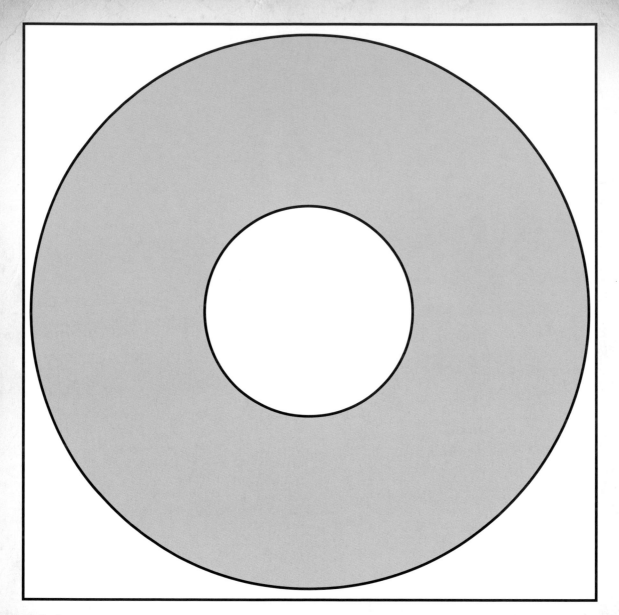

Appliqué

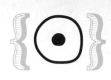 # BAD TEMPERED MAN

I got some bad scratches and bruises when I was chased off a moving hot shot train and fell. Shortly before this incident I saw three men who had unbelievable scabs on their bodies that they said they had gotten when they were kicked off a moving train on the same line. They had warned me that the railroad dicks on that line were tough, so I had that in mind when the dick rousted me out of a reefer where I was hiding. I was terrified. I tried to go down the ladder opposite the side where he stood but he pointed a revolver at me and said "Over here!" I stayed an arm's length from him, for it seemed he was ready to hit me as I moved to the other ladder. I dodged past him and jumped from the top of the boxcar but close enough to the rungs of the ladder to reach back and grab them below the top so he could not reach me. I went down the ladder not using my feet and jumped to the ground running and tumbling on the rough ballast. I was so lucky.

— JAMES R. CARROLL,
Pennsylvania

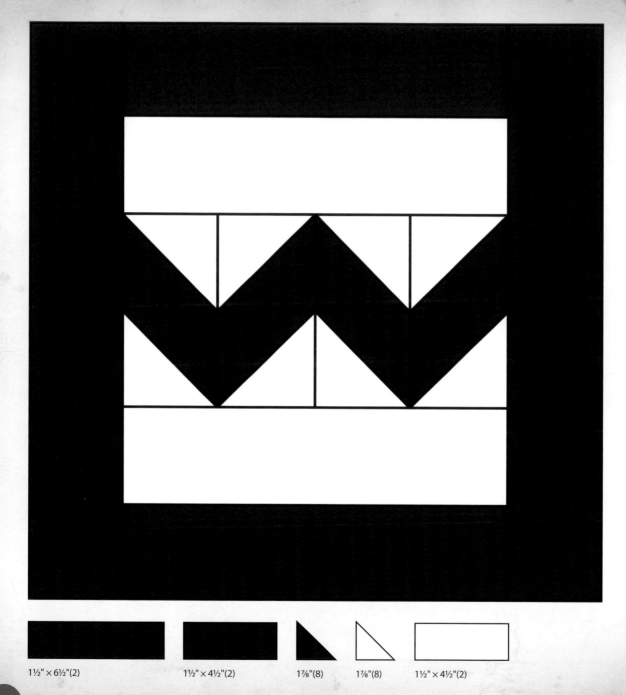

1½" × 6½"(2)   1½" × 4½"(2)   1⅞"(8)   1⅞"(8)   1½" × 4½"(2)

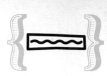

There was one lady in the neighborhood who refused to feed the "lazy bums." But everyone else did. They were concerned not with the fact that they might be lazy, but with the fact that those men were hungry, and they needed to know that there were people out there who cared. The women all said that if one of those "hobos" was their son or husband, they would like to think that some housewife was giving him a bowl of soup or a sandwich.

PATRICIA P. SCHREINER,
Michigan

29

In 1928, the bottom not only fell out of the stock market, it fell out in the Walko family: John's mother died. The twins were only a month old. John was sixteen. The same year John and his father both lost their jobs. Everybody pitched in. John knew how to make bread having helped his mother many times. Berries were picked for jelly, there was chicory coffee and for a little meat, John laid traps in the woods. Sometimes the rich (those with jobs) needed something done. That helped. It didn't bother John to knock on a door and ask. The government began a relief program. A big help.

But John was restless. And "relief" at the time carried a stigma with it. He joined the armies of men who "rode the rods." Men rode freight cars, sometimes inside, and at times on the rods along the "belly" of a freight car, looking for work, and Wall was a natural dropping off place. Wall was a place where trains were broken up and reassembled. The men would jump off the cars and immediately lose themselves in the side streets of Wall.

As soon as new freights were made up, the men were on their way, going east or west. One day John joined them. He remembers the scary freight rides, remembers being chased by the "bulls," the long walks, the pick-ups on the highway. But none of this mattered too much; he was on his way to the promised land: New York. In John's case, his Eden turned out to be under the Brooklyn Bridge.

Looking back on that little period of his life, John is glad to have experienced it. "Can't beat the camaraderie," he says. Everybody shared, everybody equal. They scrounged during the day, met in the evening around a fire, then slept until morning, to scrounge again; the old timer teaching the new.

He remembers stealing some fish from an open market. "You go," he was told. "You're young. They won't bother you."

But the nights were cold. He had no extra clothing. Besides, he didn't like the stealing part. He decided on the long trek back to home.

A Greek, driving from New York to New Jersey to visit some relatives gave him a ride as far as Reading, Pennsylvania. From there he walked. No rides. Looking back he knows why. He was dirty.

He remembers drinking some water from a stream, then washing his face, drying it with his shirt tails, left flapping in the breeze to dry out.

He remembers seeing the tip of a house over a knob. A farm house he thought. Maybe they have something to eat. He hadn't eaten for two days. Not since he left the bridge. He could almost smell the food. Maybe if he asked. Quickly he crossed the field.

Not until he knocked on the door did he see anyone. A lady opened the door, but before he could say a word she ordered him off the porch. "Get out," she cried. With a broom in her hand she almost pushed him off.

John cried to her that he's hungry; that he'd do anything for some food. "I'll work," he cried. "Anything."

"Just go," she cried. "No riff-raff around here." And John went. But only until he was out of sight.

After what he thought was a reasonable time he stole around to the back of the house. He might find something in their garden, or in a garbage dump. What he found though were cans of milk cooling in a trough. Picking up one of the metal containers, he carried it to a cherry tree, propped the can in the crook of the tree, climbed up, and feasted on milk and cherries. (He carried a collapsible tin cup. Everybody had them.)

When he finished, he carried the rest back to the trough, filled his pockets with cherries, and stole away toward the highway. But that night he vowed, "Never again will I steal to eat."

— ANN WALKO (JOHN'S WIFE),
Pennsylvania

PHOTOGRAPH BY BAIN NEWS SERVICE, COURTESY OF THE LIBRARY OF CONGRESS, LC-DIG-GGBAIN-00408

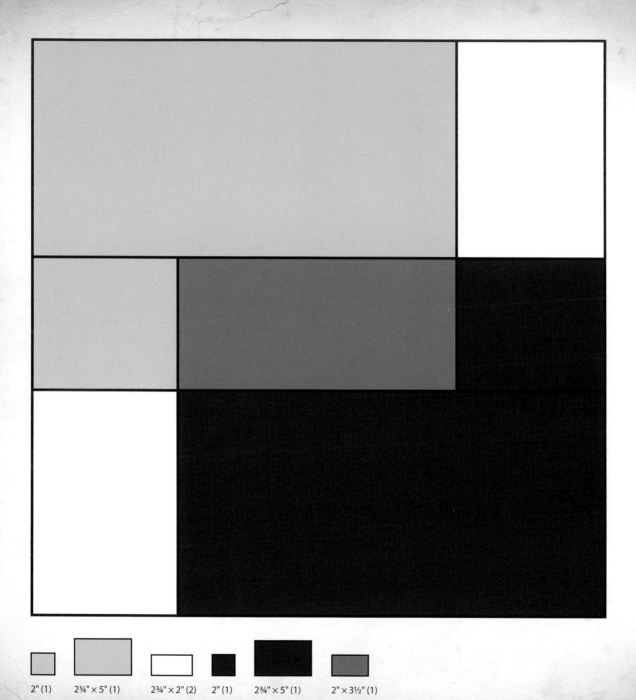

2" (1)   2¾" × 5" (1)   2¾" × 2" (2)   2" (1)   2¾" × 5" (1)   2" × 3½" (1)

Traveling north near Marysville, California, I stopped in a hobo jungle in the woods near the railroad. It was a beautiful spot in the mountains with a stream to wash in and do the laundry. I had done some work for a grocer and he had given me some food in a gunny sack. I started a fire and began to warm up some food. A hobo nearby suggested we combine our assets and have a real meal. He showed me what he had and it looked like a bargain so we whipped up an attractive meal. He made a hash dish that was very good which I ate very slowly. Fortunately, by this time I was extremely cautious and trusted nobody. I watched every move he made but saw nothing suspicious except he seemed to be watching me as we ate. Then I began to feel oddly, and when I looked at him sharply I realized that he must have put something in the food. Hastily grabbing what I could of my belongings, I ran up the hill to the tracks and up the tracks until I collapsed on a pile of rails. When I recovered consciousness the sun was no longer overhead and I was still sick. I found a place to hide while I recovered and then hopped a train moving slowly up the mountain.

— James R. Carroll,
Pennsylvania

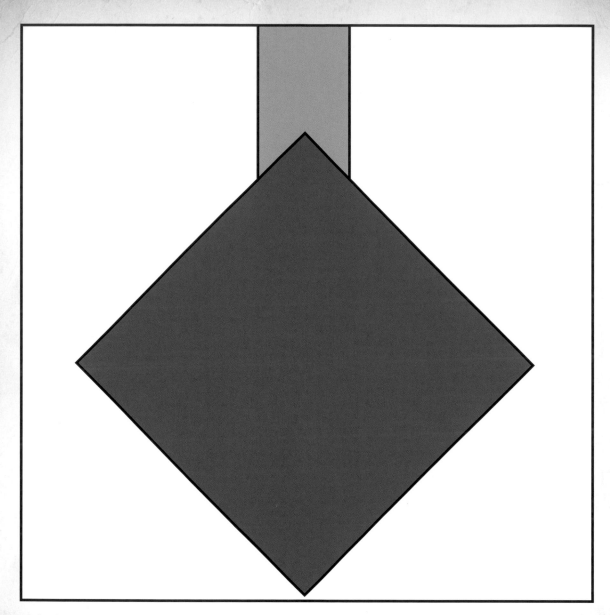

Appliqué

I happened to be around a campfire one night where "Pretty Boy Floyd" was smoking marijuana, first time that I heard it called "Loco Weed." He sat by himself, and I noticed that he was puffing with short puffs. He left for a short time, and I was told who he was and that he was a wanted man. He was dressed much better than any of those there. When he came back to sit by the fire, I was really wide-eyed watching him. I had read about him!

— BILLY A. WATKINS,
New York

I followed the harvests through the west, or wherever I could find work. The hay fields in Colorado, potato picking in Idaho, apples in Washington, hops in Oregon, etc. From 1935 through 1938, I learned the tricks of the road. How to grab a boxcar doing thirty miles per hour, how to walk on top of a train doing fifty, what not to ride on, and never, never get friendly with anyone.

Somewhere in the Montana mountains, the noisy mallet engine came to a screeching halt on a side track. A variety of men and kids climbed down off the cars. I wandered back to the jungle camp, where a fire was burning, coffee was being made, and men were sitting around on boxes, or on the ground talking. A train whistle way off around the bend alerted everyone and a five-year-old boy said "Dad, here comes our train." The train slowed down as it passed through the switch yard and everyone got aboard.

The next day we traveled until late in the afternoon, and since it was my second day without eating, I was getting desperate. Every man that crawled off that train bummed everyone they saw for food, money or anything they could get. It was really embarrassing to me as I couldn't do such a thing. I stood on the street corner watching them, when an old lady walked up and said "You poor boy, here's a dime to get a cup of coffee and a donut." I know I turned red as a beet, being so embarrassed, but was able to thank her and hurried down the street.

I was just finishing my second cup of coffee when I saw two bums had looked in the window and spotted me. I had stayed too long. When I left they followed, so I stopped and let them catch up. They said they knew that no one had any luck panhandling and wanted money to get themselves something to eat. I told them I was broke but they didn't believe me, and wouldn't let me out of their sight.

It was getting dark and I knew what would happen then, so got up and went downtown with them close behind. Finally I had a plan and walked into the depot, went to the washroom, removed my dirty overalls and washed my face and hands. Rolling up my coveralls inside out, and carrying them under my arm, walked up to the ticket agent and asked when the next train was due. The ticket agent gave me the once over, along with the time and I walked over to a bench and sat down. The two characters outside were too dirty to come in, but kept looking in the window, as I sat there looking at old magazines.

The passenger train came puffing in, steam so thick visibility was zero on the platform, so I walked unnoticed toward the front of the train, and climbed up between two baggage coaches, and found room to stand in a door way. The train took off, wheels spinning, steam belching from the cylinders, whistle blowing, and I figured I had shook off the two that shadowed me all afternoon. It was no easy matter hanging on in between the cars, as the train picked up speed, and then I realized my biggest mistake, too late.

I had escaped the two that were following me, but red hot coals belching out of the smoke stack bounced along the top of the cars, fell in between, down my neck, and started fires in my clothes. That train must have been doing seventy-five miles an hour and with me beating out the fires on my clothes, and trying to hang on, it was something I don't care to dwell on very long.

The train stopped twenty miles out to take on water, the two bums were spotted on the coal car and kicked off. They shook their fists at me, as the train took off, and I gave them my best victory smile. The place where the train took on water had just a large water tank, called a "jerk water," with no other buildings around, and trains may not stop there again for day, making it the worst place for bums to be kicked off.

DONALD E. NEWHOUSER,
Indiana

Photograph by Dorothea Lange, Courtesy of the Library of Congress, lc-dig-fsa-8b33263

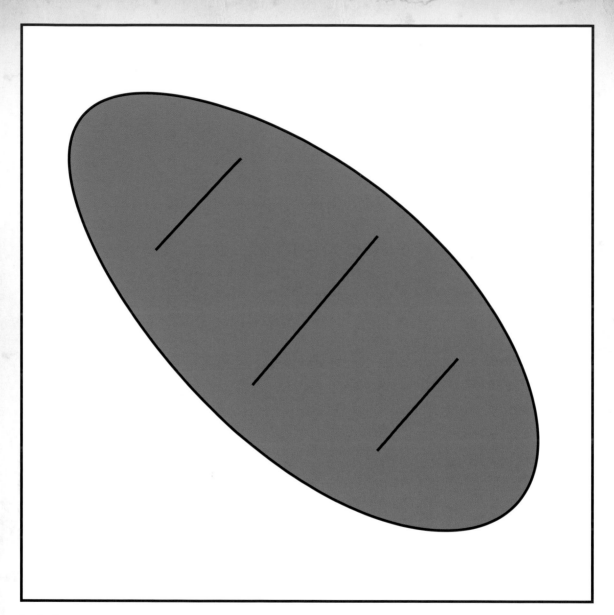

Appliqué

{🍞} BREAD

There were many "hobos" on those trains, and many of them came to the houses in our neighborhood to beg for food. Summer saw them wearing the most tattered clothes I ever saw, and there were lots of bare feet. Winter saw them wearing a jacket over a sweater, tattered trousers, and shoes full of holes, and the soles flapped loose as they walked. Some wore overcoats that were ragged, and the lining hung below the hemlines. Most of them had no boots on their feet—only the loose-soled shoes that flapped. On their hands, most had gloves, only the fingers were all raveled out. These men were hungry, and they were dirty, but not one of them ever behaved in any but the politest manner, and all they asked for was something to eat. My mother, and all the other women in that neighborhood, always gave them food, even if it wasn't always much more than a sandwich. The sandwiches always disappeared in a big hurry, too.

PATRICIA P. SCHREINER,
Michigan

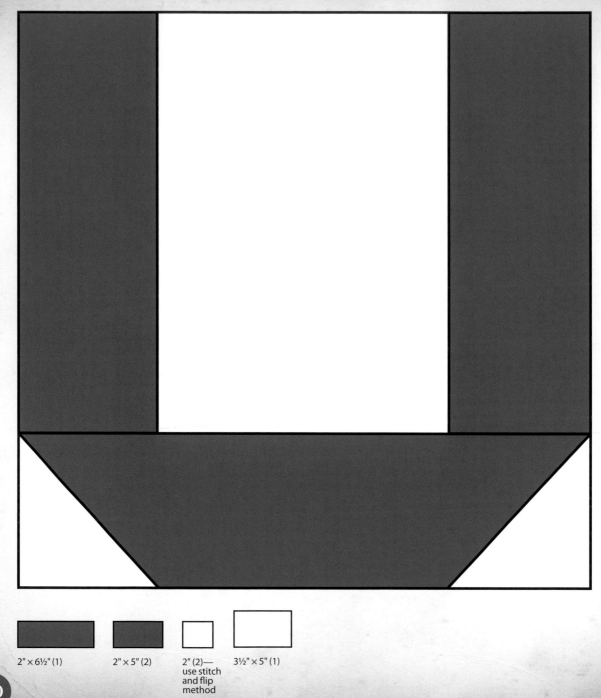

2" × 6½" (1)

2" × 5" (2)

2" (2)—
use stitch
and flip
method

3½" × 5" (1)

Many hobos would end up in this isolated area; somewhat of a dead end street to be stranded. However maybe intended to, for the sand house was a haven for some. It was a large basement full of sand. A railroad track above supported cars, and sand was unloaded through hatches in this building and provided a dark area where you could sleep and hide behind piles of sand. Two steam dryers provided heat.

— MICHAEL CORINCHOCK,
Pennsylvania

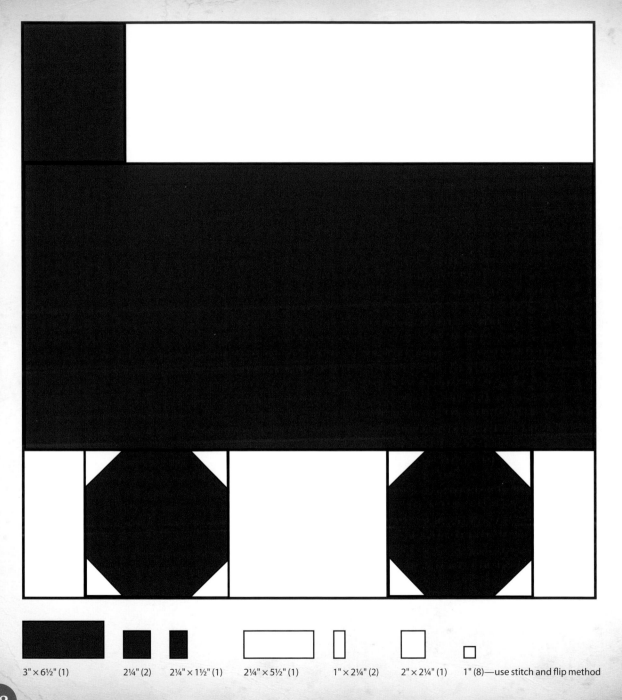

3" × 6½" (1)   2¼" (2)   2¼" × 1½" (1)   2¼" × 5½" (1)   1" × 2¼" (2)   2" × 2¼" (1)   1" (8)—use stitch and flip method

I was raised near the town of Greybull, Wyoming. Among other things it was a railroad town. There was a roundhouse where locomotives were repaired; the train changed crews there; there were the section crews and railroad detectives.

I know that the northbound freights came to an almost complete stop near the south boundary of the city and all the non fare paying passengers jumped off. I have to believe the so called "railroad bulls" went through the trains and rounded up the trespassers. The same was probably true of the southbound trains.

Of the people that departed south of town, they would walk through the town. North of the town the engineer would slow the train down and "Knights of the Road" would jump on. The people who lived in the first house the hobos would reach told my parents one day ninety-six people came to their door asking for a handout. They were hoping for four more to make it an even hundred.

— DON RODGERS,
California

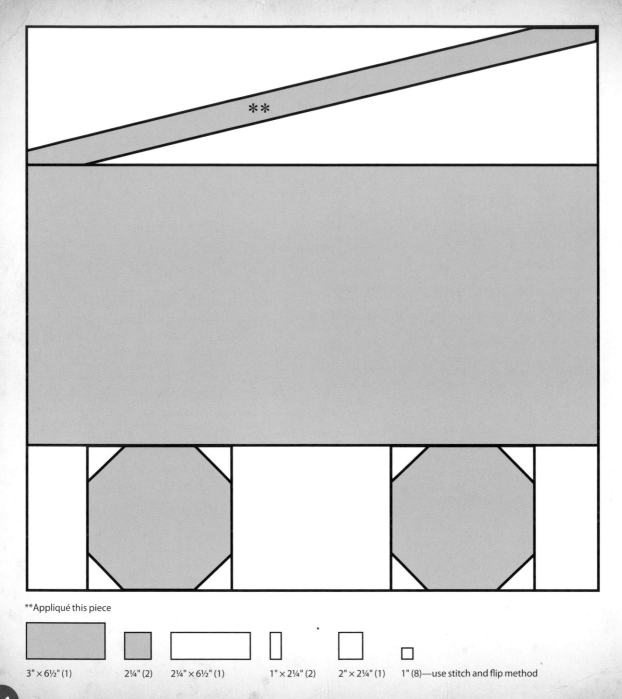

**

**Appliqué this piece

3" × 6½" (1)	2¼" (2)	2¼" × 6½" (1)	1" × 2¼" (2)	2" × 2¼" (1)	1" (8)—use stitch and flip method

I was riding a passenger train one night in between the cars when a railroad detective spotted me. I jumped on the other side and climbed on top of the train. The train rolled out of the station and I had to ride 100 miles holding on for dear life. Every time we took a curve, I would slide toward the edge. I prayed a lot.

ARCHIE FROST,
Missouri

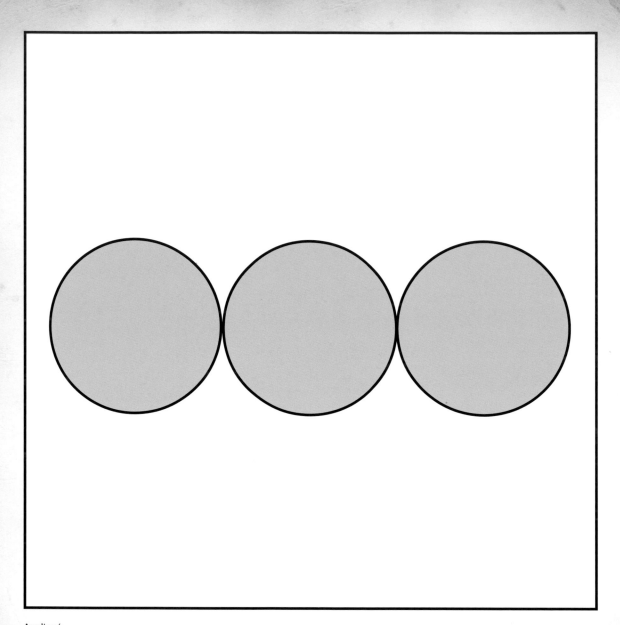

Appliqué

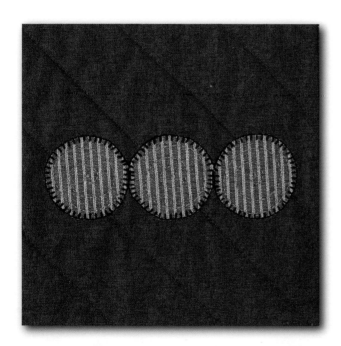

Going through Georgia, my blood ran cold every time that I saw a police car. It was against the law to hitchhike there, and if you were caught, it meant 30 days on the dreaded chain gang.

— PAUL BOOKER,
California

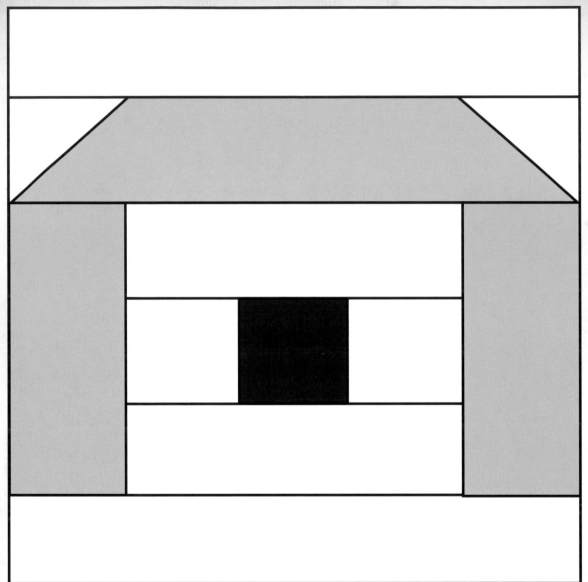

Reversing this block reverses this meaning: Rotate the block 180 degrees for the sign "Cops Inactive."

1½" × 6½" (1) 1½" × 3½" (2) 1½" (1) 1½" × 6½" (2) 1½" × 4½" (2) 1½" × 2" (2) 1½" (2)—use stitch and flip method

In a small Texas town near the border, the train was stopped by the Border Patrol and police looking for Mexicans. We were all told to get off, but the residents were marching up and down on both sides of the train with pick handles and clubs, shouting to us "not to get off, there was no work for us there." There were more of us than residents of the town, but we stayed on the right-a-way, leaning on the cars until the Patrol found the three Mexicans and let the train move on.

— BILLY A. WATKINS,
Indiana

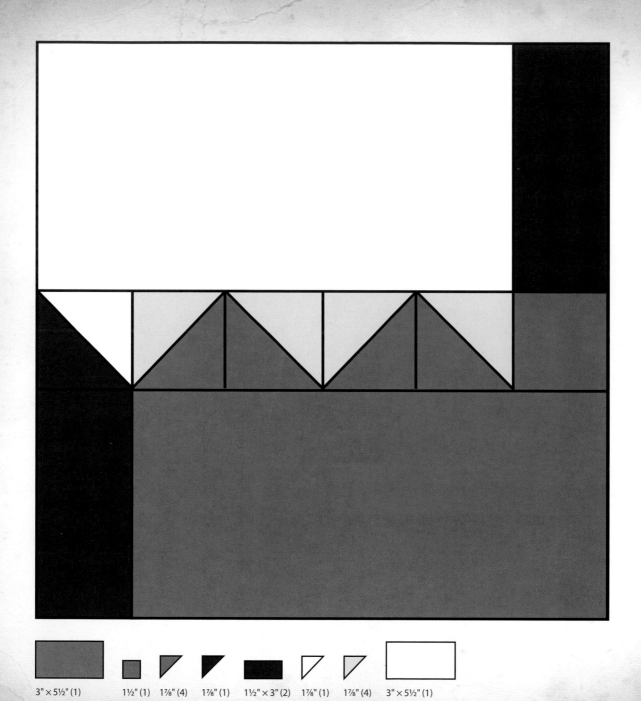

3" × 5½" (1)   1½" (1)   1⅞" (4)   1⅞" (1)   1½" × 3" (2)   1⅞" (1)   1⅞" (4)   3" × 5½" (1)

In the early hour of the morning west of Laramie, Wyoming, it got pretty cold and while we were stopped, way out in the middle of nowhere, I hopped out and gathered up a big bunch of Canadian thistle, or tumbleweed. They were tough and springy and grew in a big ball. I used them to make a bed and they helped soften the floor quite a bit. Along about daylight, I woke up and rolled a cigarette and while I had the match lit, I pulled off a piece of that tumble weed and set it afire. When it was about out, I dropped it on the floor of the boxcar and added another small piece. In nothing flat, there was four or five fellows standing and squatting around that little fire. Someone else added a sprig or two … the next thing we knew the floor of the boxcar was on fire, so we stomped it out, but we could see fire down in a crack where the wind was fanning it. We sure thought we were in trouble. I know I imagined what was going to happen to us if that car burned. We could see jail very plain. There was nothing for it, but to use the only source of water we had, so each man stepped up and peed every drop possible, and low and behold, the fire was out. Needless to say, we didn't start any more fires. No one wanted to be stranded way out in the middle of that high desert.

— GORDON AYRES,
California

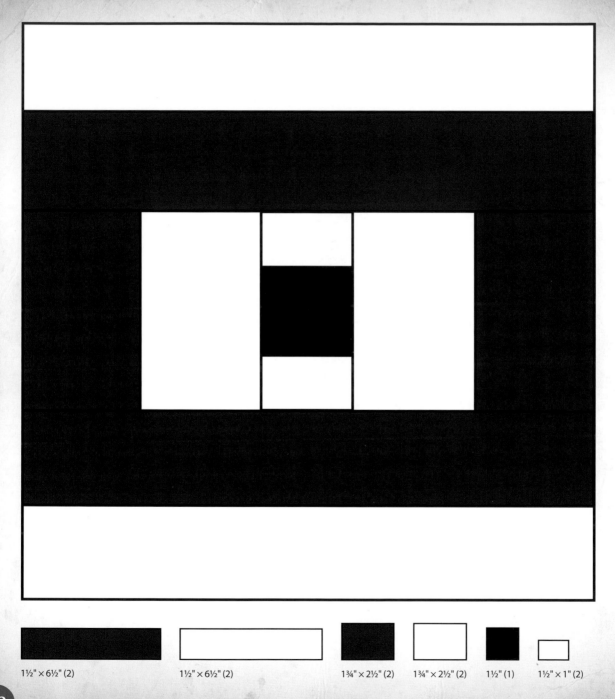

1½" × 6½" (2) 1½" × 6½" (2) 1¾" × 2½" (2) 1¾" × 2½" (2) 1½" (1) 1½" × 1" (2)

{ ▫ } DANGER

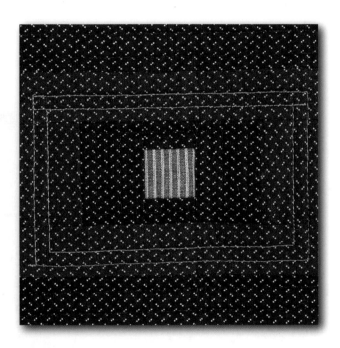

uncan, Oklahoma, 1938. I was staying with a brother when I decided to go to California. I was standing beside the tracks, with my worldly possessions in a shoe box, tied with a string. With my arm through the string I caught a freight running rather fast. The string broke, and I lost my shoe box. I jumped back off and landed with my face in crushed rock. A man in a car saw me and took me to a doctor. My wrapped head looked like a mummy. I went back to my brother's house. I still have some of the scars.

— James L. Blackman,
Missouri

Two young boys and myself were riding together on top a freight car out of Cheyenne, Wyoming. As night approached we sought protection from the cold in a reefer because we could not find an empty car. We all fell asleep, I guess, and then I awoke to a ghost-like silence. I felt like I was disembodied in another world. When I tried to move it was as though I had no strength. I knew something was terribly wrong and I finally managed to sit up. I could see some faint light through the reefer door above and struggled to the ladder and climbed up until my shoulders were outside. After a bit I realized that we had stopped in a rail yard and there was no activity at all. I called to the other boys but got no answer. A call for help was futile. Panic seized me and I went down and tried to awaken them. They seemed to be dead but I continued to talk to them and move them around. One of them gave signs of life and was finally revived. Together we got the other one up and out on the ground. We staggered out to a highway and down to an all night lunchroom where we got warmth and some hot drinks. We picked up a Rawlings newspaper lying on the counter and read it. The headline said the bodies of two boys had been found in a reefer where they had died from hyperthermia. The realization that we had come so close to death showed on our faces.

— JAMES R. CARROLL,
Pennsylvania

Photograph by John Vachon, Courtesy of the Library of Congress, lc-usz62-129928

1¼" × 6½" (2)   2" × 1½" (2)   1" × 1½" (1)   2⅜" (8)   1½" × 1" (2)   1" × 6½" (1)   1" × 1½" (2)   2⅜" (8)

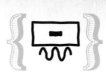

DANGEROUS DRINKING WATER

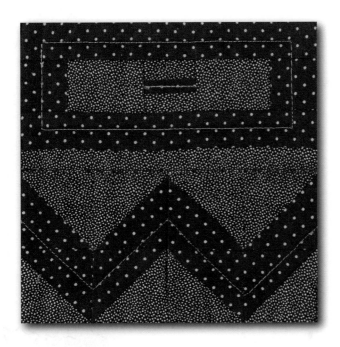

I traveled through Nebraska and Kansas the year the grasshoppers were so bad, they left nothing standing in their path. They were so bad some places cars would stall on hills in the road. You would have to stop every few miles to clean your windshield. That was, I think 1935. That was the year the drought was real bad in Iowa. I worked for a while for a farmer in Bramer, Colorado. I remember while I was there he shipped a bog old boar hog to market. He received one penny per pound for the hog. I believe at that time top price for hogs were four or five cents per pound. That, my friend, was hard times.

CHARLES RANKIN,
Ohio

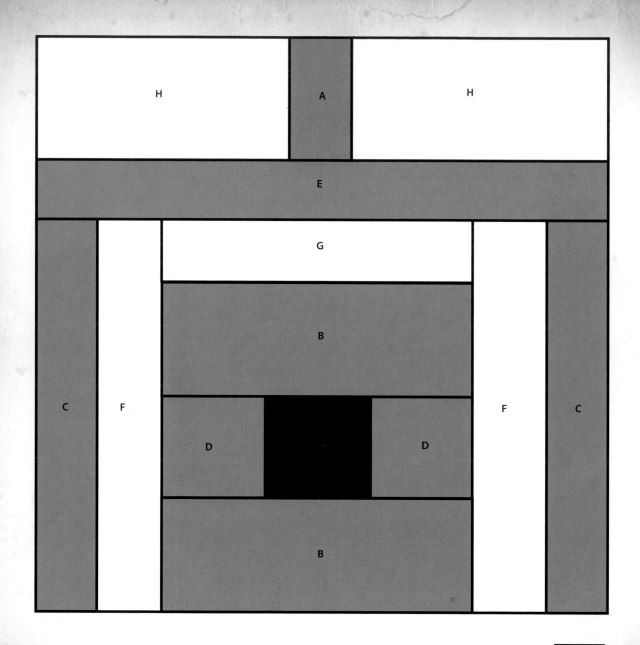

 A
1½" × 2" (1)

 B
1½" × 3½" (2)

 C
1¼" × 4¼" (2)

 D
1½" (2)

 **E**
1¼" × 6½" (1)

 F
1¼" × 4¼" (2)

G
1 ¼" × 3½" (1)

H
2" × 3" (2)

1½" (1)

In those days one saw a few true hobos but by and large most everyone we met were people going somewhere to find work or returning home. One ran into all sorts of railroad personnel, some would advise you which train to catch and where to catch it while others would threaten you. Once in Council Bluffs, Iowa, someone actually shot at us, at least close enough we heard the bullets ricochet around us.

— BUD HUGHES,
Nebraska

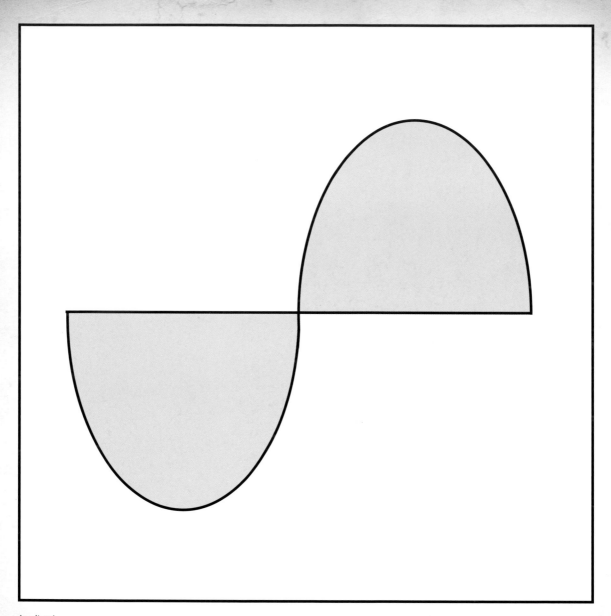

Appliqué

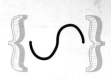

DISHONEST PERSON LIVES HERE

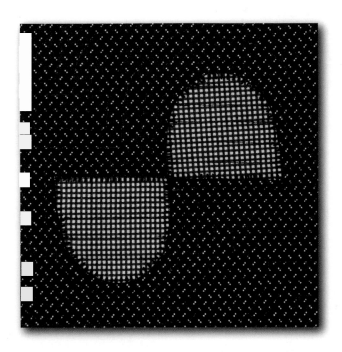

There just were not any work to be had, for anyone to find a job, you had to be lucky. One had to be at the right place at the right time. When you did find a factory open, there were always lots of people standing around at the gate, looking for work. The pay in those days just left a lot to be desired. I did a lot of work in those days just for board lodging. I worked for an old farmer in upstate New York once, we helped him make hay for three days. When we finished the job, he refused to pay us for our work. He claimed that we didn't work hard enough, and that we should not complain, that he had given us food and a place to stay for three days. When we put up a beef he threatened to call the State Police. He told us that because we were on the road, that the cops would not believe us and that we would get in trouble. In most cases like that, he was right. So we just moved on.

— CHARLES RANKIN,
Ohio

If desired, use buttons and embroidery floss to embellish the face on the block.

1½" × 6½" (1)   1½" × 3" (2)   3" (1)   3" (3)   1¼" (4)—use stitch and flip method

DOCTOR, NO CHARGE

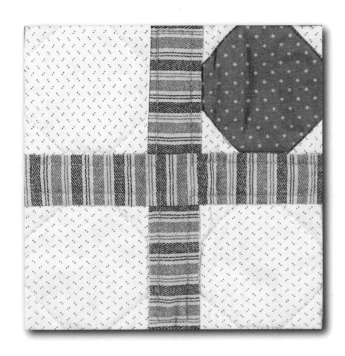

One time I got a cinder in my eye. I had perfect eyesight and could see it. The first doctor I went to could not see it. The second doctor located, removed it and would not take a dime even though at the time he did not have much.

— MALCOLM D. STEWART,
Indiana

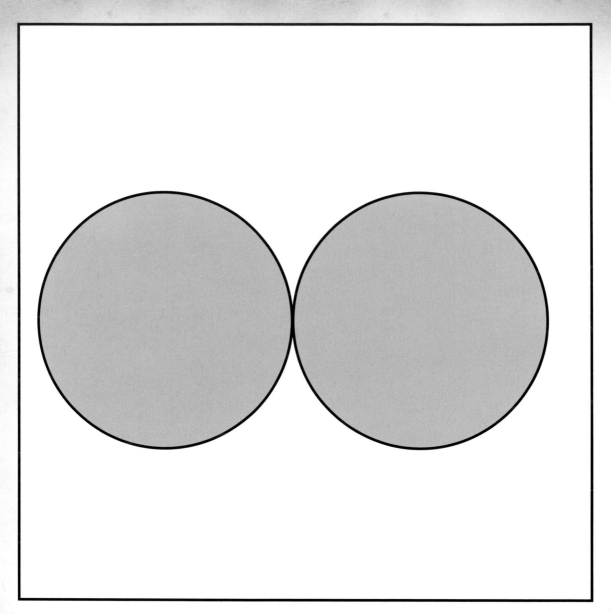

Appliqué

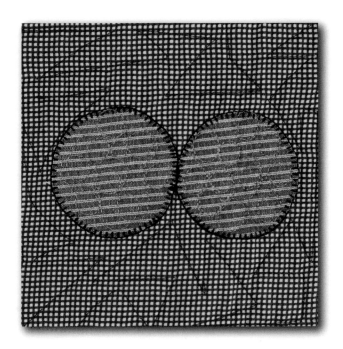

The year was 1931. My younger brother and I were walking along the railroad tracks which were a short distance from our small farm. We each had a bucket looking for chunks of coal that might have fallen from a passing coal car. We could hear a train approaching in the distance so we went down the embankment and waited for the train to pass. There were freight cars and sitting on top of one of the boxcars. From his perch he could see us with our buckets and immediately jumped up and ran down the row of boxcars until he came to a coal car. He started throwing chunks of coal down to us as fast as he could before the train reached the next crossing.

How happy we were that we could fill our buckets up. There was someone who understood—and cared.

— HARRIET DICKENSON,
Indiana

65

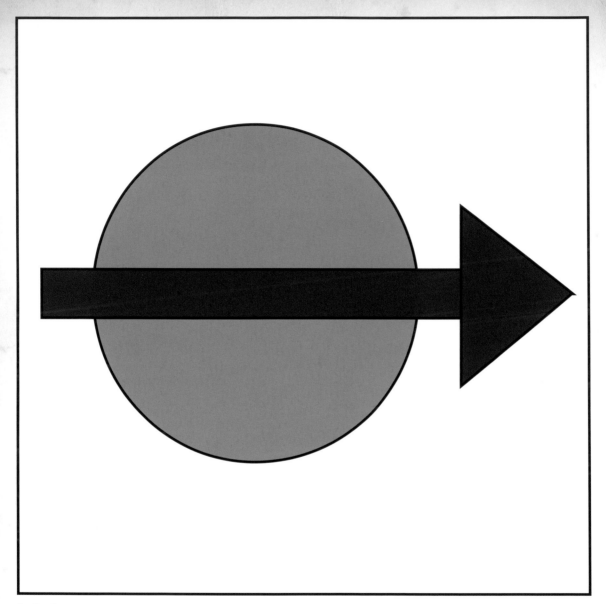

Appliqué

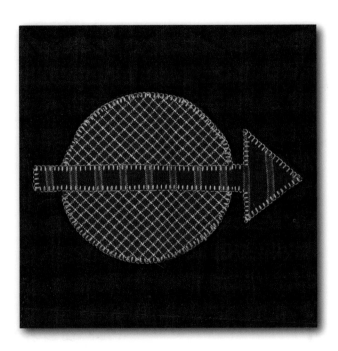

We walked through town knocking on doors for handouts and wound up on the west side of Cheyenne at 7:00 or 8:00 in the evening. A fairly short freight came puffing up the long grade and we prepared to "jump it." It's not an easy thing to do even though it's traveling fairly slow. We had a suitcase to carry and still try with one hand to grab a rung of the ladder on the side of the car. After stepping and falling and missing several times we managed to climb aboard—up the ladder to the top of the car. By this time the train was picking up speed and we had to lay flat on the top spread-eagled to keep from falling off. For over four hours we clung to the top of this "hi-balling" freight hoping it would eventually slow down at some division point. This was a coal burning engine (two of them), so the smoke and soot came straight back plastering us unmercifully. We wound up in Evanston, Wyoming, thankful to get off in one piece. We found a YMCA where we stayed, showering for an hour to get rid of the smoke and soot.

— VICTOR MARTENS,
Indiana

We had already learned the names of the different kinds of cars. Refrigerator cars were dangerous because if you got locked into one you could suffocate. Furniture cars usually had paper strewn around in which you could make a bed but they were so high that they swayed, which was uncomfortable. Flat cars and gondolas were so light when empty that they jumped around, etc.

After our long discussion, we were hungry and we had no money. "Just go over to that store," he said. "Tell them that you are broke and hungry and they will give you something. Here I'll show you."

He went into the store and soon came back with some stale rolls. Then Jim went in and came back with more stale rolls. Next it was my turn. There were two older men sitting in the back of the store in deep conversation. I hesitatingly walked back and gave my sorrowful pitch.

"By Gad," one of them said, "you are the third one in here in the last ten minutes." He got up and cut a chunk of cheese from a large daisy and put it in a sack with some crackers. As I walked out the door he handed me an over-ripe melon. I thanked him profusely and joined the others.

"Hey, you did great," was my greeting. We found a place to sit to enjoy our feast. A man came by and Jim asked him if he had a smoke. He gave Jim a cigar. As we started back to the station Jim lit the cigar and strutted out in front uf us. Pandemonium broke loose. We were passing a red-light district and when the girls saw him they rapped on windows and called to him. One of them came out and led him into the house. When he came out we asked him what he did in there.

"I told them I was hungry and did they have anything to eat and they kicked me out."

CHARLES N. BISHOP,
California

PHOTOGRAPH BY DOROTHEA LANGE, COURTESY OF THE LIBRARY OF CONGRESS, LC-USF34-016104

69

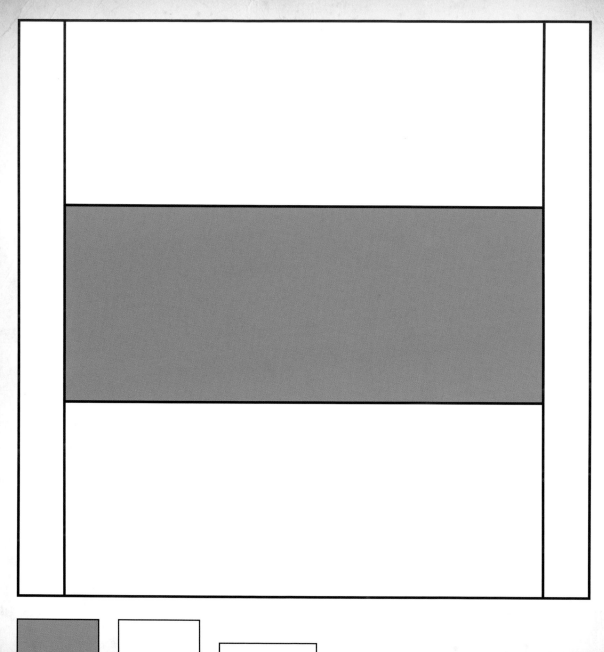

2½" × 5½" (1)   2½" × 5½" (2)   1" × 6½" (2)

{—} DOUBTFUL

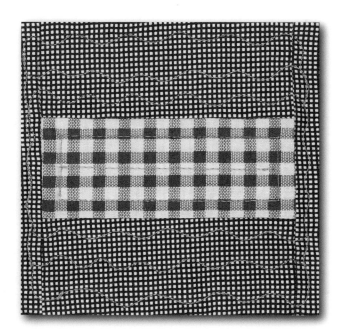

If you don't think it's a thrill walking twenty tops of boxcars after dark with the train running thirty-five miles an hour, jumping from one car to the other car. One missed jump and you fall between the cars.

— FRED GRIFFIN,
Missouri

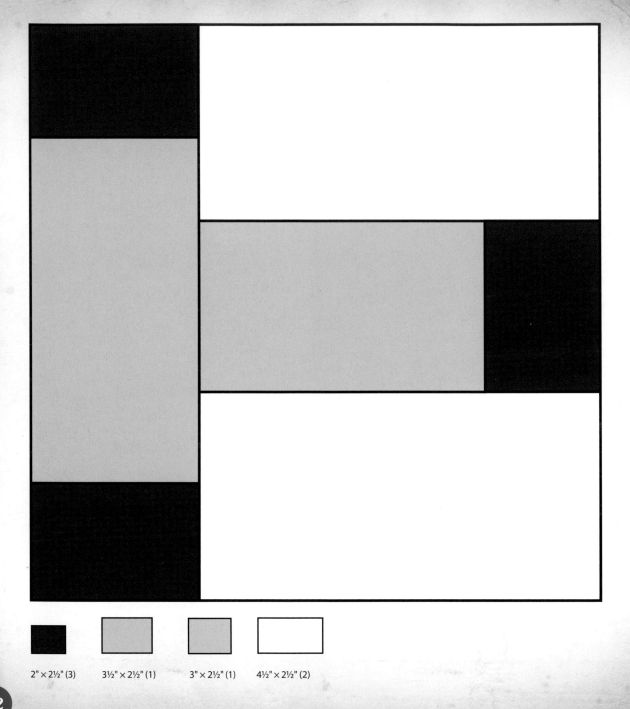

2" × 2½" (3)   3½" × 2½" (1)   3" × 2½" (1)   4½" × 2½" (2)

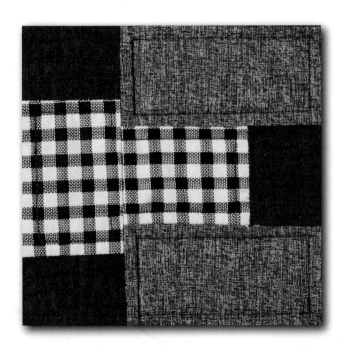

I left home when I was around 13 years old. I left because our stepmother used to beat me, my older brother and two sisters. I went door to door and asked for food. Sometimes I would go to the jailhouses and sleep there. Other times I slept in boxcars, cheap motels and when in New York, the subways. Also flophouses and missions. I begged for money which came easy because I was so young. At Miami Beach, Florida, I would beg people so I could get something to eat. One older couple gave me twenty-five cents and they were following me. They saw me go into a café. I sat at the counter and asked the waiter if he could spare me something to eat. He said yes. The couple who gave me the twenty-five cents called me out of the café. They then gave me another $2.00. In San Francisco on Nob Hill, I would go on the street at night and beg for money. It was generally damp and drizzling and I would be wearing shorts. People felt sorry for me.

WILLIAM CSONDOR,
Pennsylvania

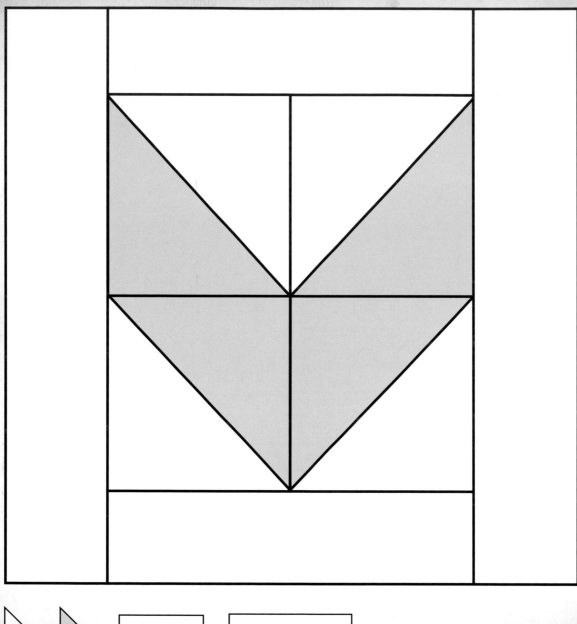

2⅞" (4)   2⅞" (4)   1½" × 4½" (2)   1½" × 6½" (2)

We would ask other bums where the empties were and if they were enclosed we would take them. Some cars had pretty rank odors, others were fairly clean. We felt ourselves fortunate if there was paper in the car. Paper was a wonderful insulation. It was not soft but it kept out the cold. The hard rock bum carried a bedroll and knew the rules of the railroads. He did not care which direction he went. He had been to these places before. He did, however, travel the northern states in the summer and head to the sunbelt in winter. They had nicknames like Milwaukee Red, Bullet Jo, Alabama Ray (with a southern accent) and many, many more. Our adventure west ended someplace in Idaho. At this point we had enough of cold nights, intermittent food, jerky, rough riding trains and stinking bodies (ours). The glory of being one of the knights of the road was wearing very thin. We caught a train going east and headed for home. Going east was usually easier than going the other way. Detroit shipped its automobiles enclosed in boxcars going west and going east they were taking the empty ones back to the factory. As our extra bonus they had heavy wrapping paper inside.

— RALPH H. SHIRLEY,
Montana

75

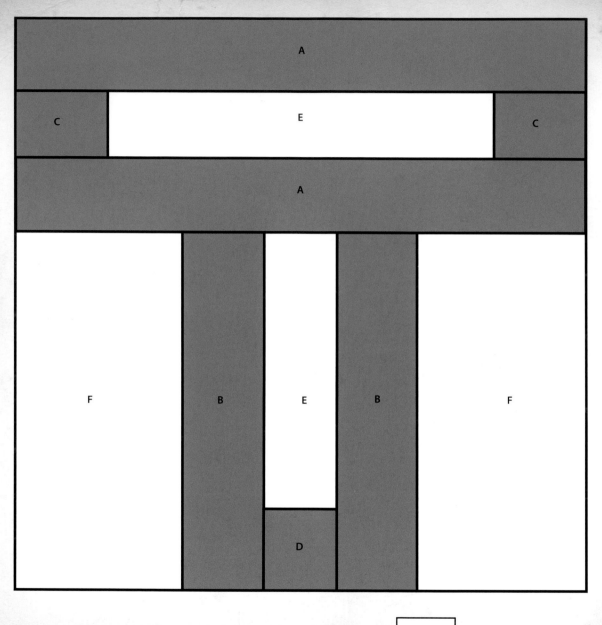

A	B	C	D	E	F
1¼" × 6½" (2)	1¼" × 4¼" (2)	1¼" × 2" (2)	1¼" × 1¼" (2)	1¼" × 3½" (2)	4¼" × 2⅜" (2)

My great Aunt Iva told me the story of my great grandmother, Jenny Foster Councilman. A hobo came to her door asking to work for food. Jenny was a great cook and was happy to oblige. He chopped a goodly amount of wood and was paid with one of her delicious meals. Soon she was getting more and more of these men and they had fixed everything she could possibly think of to get done. One day she was talking over her fence with a neighbor woman and explained what was going on. The neighbor said, "Well, Jenny, if you would take the sign off your fence in front of the house, it will stop." Jenny found the sign that, as explained to me, was some sort of cross that meant food for work. Jenny had no more hobos at her house.

— JUANITA PENMAN,
Tennessee

Appliqué

 # FREE PHONE

We always thought that on a particular tree or telephone pole on the outside of town, anyone traveling could find directions to our house for a hot meal in a warm house in winter or a cool house in summer.

If one of us kids saw ragged looking people on the porch or walk we would tell mom, then we'd scoot out of the way. They would knock, mom would answer and say "Yes, I'll get it ready and you can come in." Food was served family style, so they could take as much or as little as they wanted. All home canned food, home-made bread and hot coffee. Sometimes they'd ask and take a sandwich with them.

Dad worked for Superior Sheet Steel in Louisville, Ohio. Being a family of 6, they made sure he had 2 days work in any 2 week period. Any time a farmer killed a cow we got a big roast. We didn't have much, but we knew we had a lot more than the people who stopped by. We children had a name for them: "Weary Willies."

— RUBY LeMUNYAN,
California

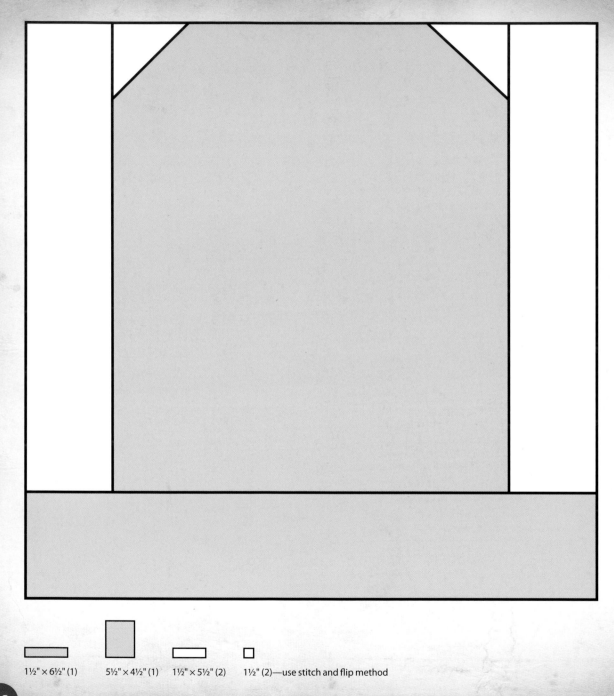

1½" × 6½" (1)   5½" × 4½" (1)   1½" × 5½" (2)   1½" (2)—use stitch and flip method

{🎩} GENTLEMAN

I was in a jungle one time and a short heavy bum was singing with a beautiful voice. He sang ballads and railroad songs. Called himself the Way Faring Stranger. I found out later it was Burl Ives.

H.B. "Down the Road Doc" Harmon,
California

I arrived in Fargo this evening after a freight train ride on the Chicago & North-Western railroad from Ortonville, Minnesota. As I walked on a street (Broadway) I waited as a Great Northern freight train was blocking the street. A neatly dressed young-looking fellow struck up a conversation as we waited and I explained I had arrived from Ohio, still looking for work in the harvest fields. This was a drought year and the grain crop was far below par, so I had trouble even getting enough to eat.

As the train passed, we continued down the street and as we passed the Hotel Powers, he asked if I was hungry. Of course I was, but when he started to take me into the coffee shop I told him I was dirty and didn't think I should go in there. I was glad he insisted, so I went in with him. He gave some instructions to a pretty red-headed waitress, then he left me there to eat. I was served a 50 cent chicken dinner complete with dessert. In 1933, a 50 cent dinner was a regular banquet.

When I asked the waitress about the man she said, "That's my boss, Mr. Powers. He runs this hotel."

He had also instructed her to give me a room for the night, and I was taken to room 212. The next morning, I was told breakfast was waiting for me in the coffee shop. I had never stayed in a hotel in my life so it was an experience. He gave me more than food and a place to say. He gave me dignity.

— ROGER BROWN,
Ohio

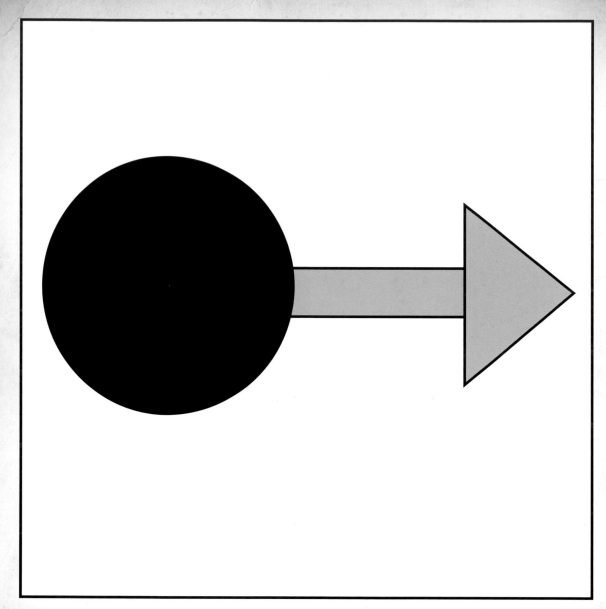

Appliqué

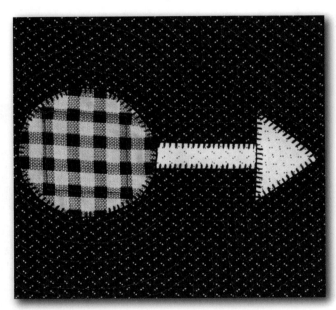

The most spectacular sight that I have ever seen was at least a thousand men sitting, if they could find a space, atop this mile long freight train. They were headed for California, looking for work, any kind of work, even for fifty cents a day.

— PAUL BOOKER,
California

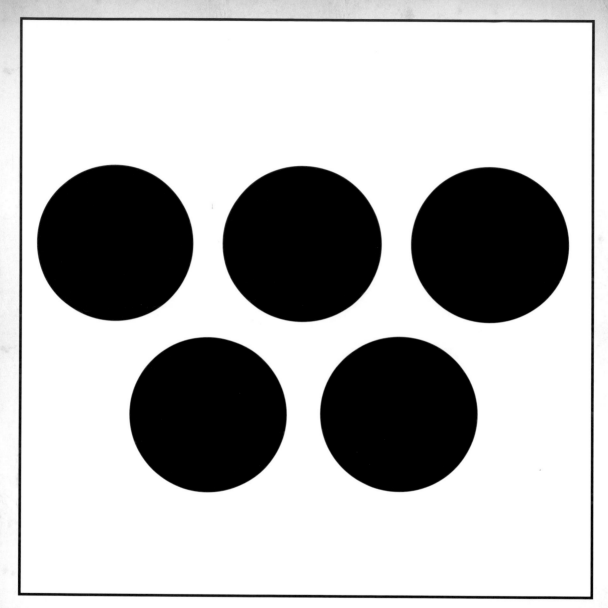

Appliqué

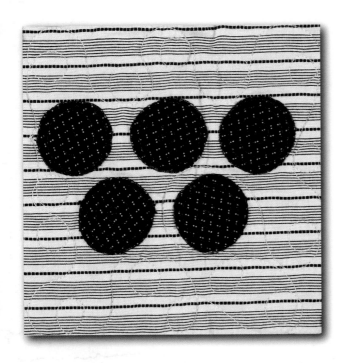

Just go where the work was. I topped beets, picked spuds, put up hay, and plowed with a six horse team. I logged in California. That's where I got my first job that paid $1 an hour. Before that it was a dollar or two a day.

— LYLE A. O'HARE,
Nebraska

 3⅞" (4)

 1½" (4)—use stitch and flip method

2" (4)—use stitch and flip method

2¼" (4)

 4¾" × 1¼" (1)

 2¼" × 1¼" (2)

Another time after not eating for two days I stopped at a small grocery store hoping to bum some food. As I stepped in the doorway a woman followed me in. I motioned to the grocer to wait on her first. She was a cash customer and I was just a 'bo. The grocer put a few things on the counter she ordered and without a warning threw a brown bag at me. He knew what I was there for. I stammered my thanks and as I stepped out on the side walk and looked down, I saw the familiar chalk mark there stating to all 'bos that the grocer was a kind hearted, soft touch. The bag held sandwiches, a cake and an apple.

— Frank Kriech,
Ohio

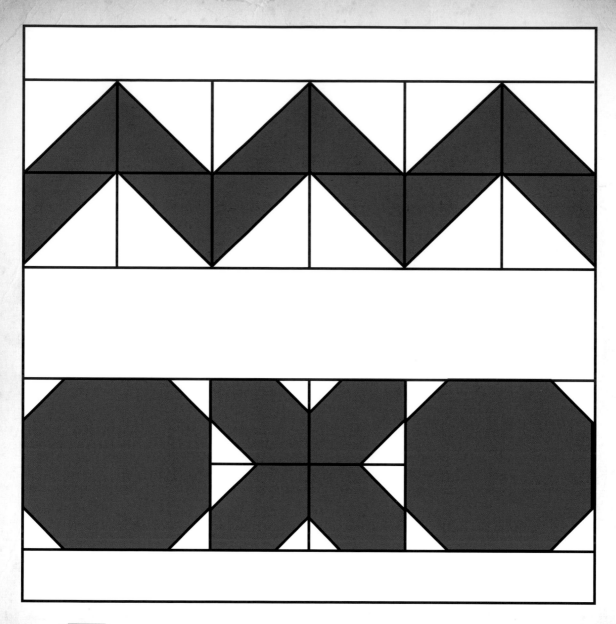

    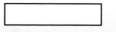

1⅞" (12)   2½" (2)   1½" (4)   1" x 6½" (2)   1½" x 6½" (1)   1⅞" (12)   1" (16)—use stitch and flip method

Started with $24 and worked a few hours selling papers and on odd jobs. Ate in soup kitchens and bummed on street or at food stores. In less populated ares, I carried a little gunny sack with things like peanut butter, bread, sardines or baked beans which I bought or for which I did some work. Slept in or on freight cars, in hay stacks if lucky, in the woods, in hobo camps, in the field, in a rented room near the Olympic area for a week, in vacant buildings or shelters and, once, unknowingly, on a dung heap under a loading platform. Sanitary, bathing and laundry needs were fulfilled any way possible. Veteran hobos knew all the spots where good water was available so I followed them when possible. We seemed always to be looking for water.

— JAMES R. CARROLL,
Pennsylvania

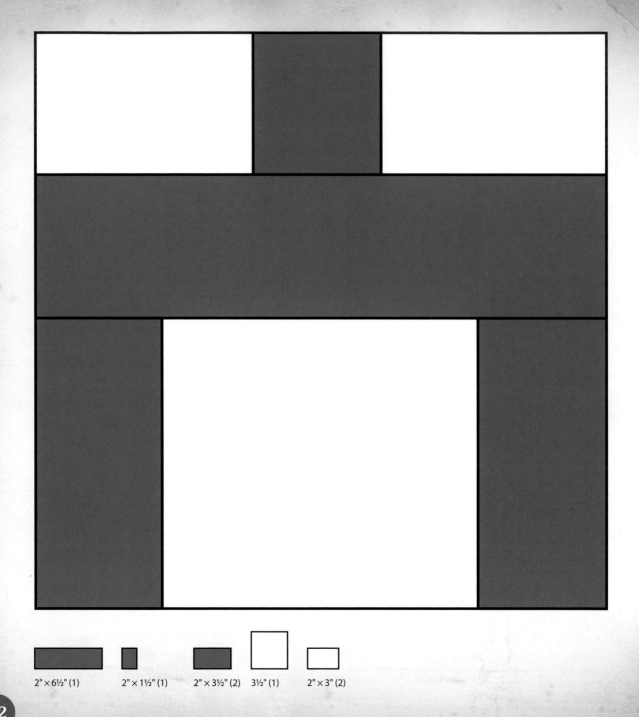

2" × 6½" (1) 2" × 1½" (1) 2" × 3½" (2) 3½" (1) 2" × 3" (2)

We boarded the train at night at Julesburg, Colorado. All that we could find open for us was a gondola car, filled with rocks, in which we made ourselves as comfortable as possible. Our gondola was 3 or 4 cars behind the locomotive and as the train picked up speed (as high as eighty mph) the sparks from the engine flew over our heads like a shower of fireworks.

— Jesse M. Elson,
Pennsylvania

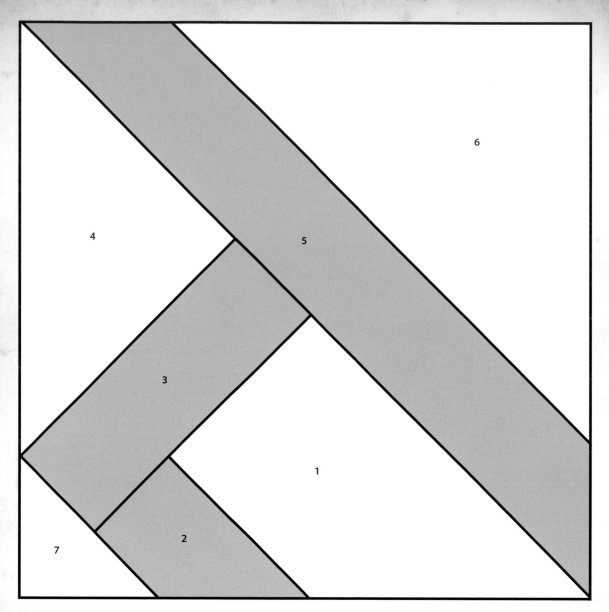

Paper piece

The rail bulls had a program in Pomona, California whereby they got on the train—both front and back—the train then speeded up and the detectives converged toward the middle of the train at which time you could jump or be thrown off the speeding train. I chose to jump and entered the outskirts of Los Angeles, "The Land of Milk and Honey."

— MARION ALVIN ALLEY,
California

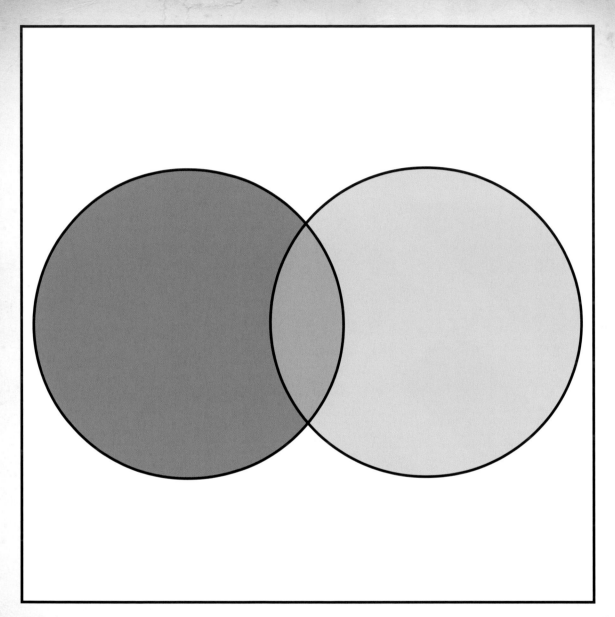

Appliqué

At Yuma, Arizona, I hopped a train on the old San Diego and Arizona Railroad. I didn't know that it dipped into Mexico two times. I was riding in between two boxcars, when as we pulled into Mexicala, I saw two soldiers, one on each side of the train, rifles in hand, looking for hobos. I had visions of the dreaded Mexican calaboose, which I had heard terrible tales about. I lucked out and wasn't discovered, because one soldier was one boxcar ahead of the one on the other side. I hid down by the wheels on one side, then on the other side, as the other soldier came by.

— PAUL BOOKER,
California

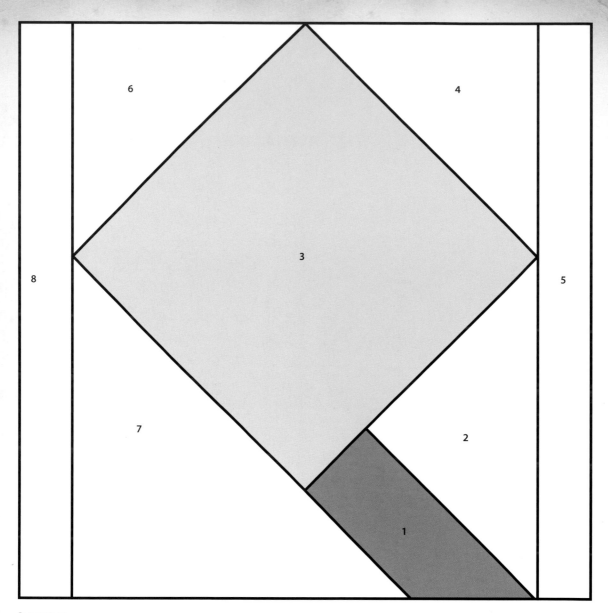

Paper piece

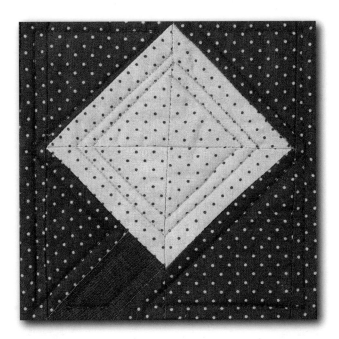

In a Hobo Jungle under a bridge near the rail yards near Klamath Falls, Oregon, I met an old fella who had lost his leg riding the rails. Next morning I caught a freight bound for Sparks, Nevada. I was on a flat car as the train started to pull out when here came the one-legged gent. I extended my arm. He took my hand and swung onto the flatcar. We sat side-by-side for a few miles before I felt like talking. "How did you get started on the bum, anyway?" I asked for openers. He gave me a long and steady look. Then he said: "You'll learn sooner or later that there are some questions you have no right to ask." We didn't talk much after that but in the ensuing years, I have thanked the old gent for that sage advice.

— MORRIS M. THOMTE,
Arizona

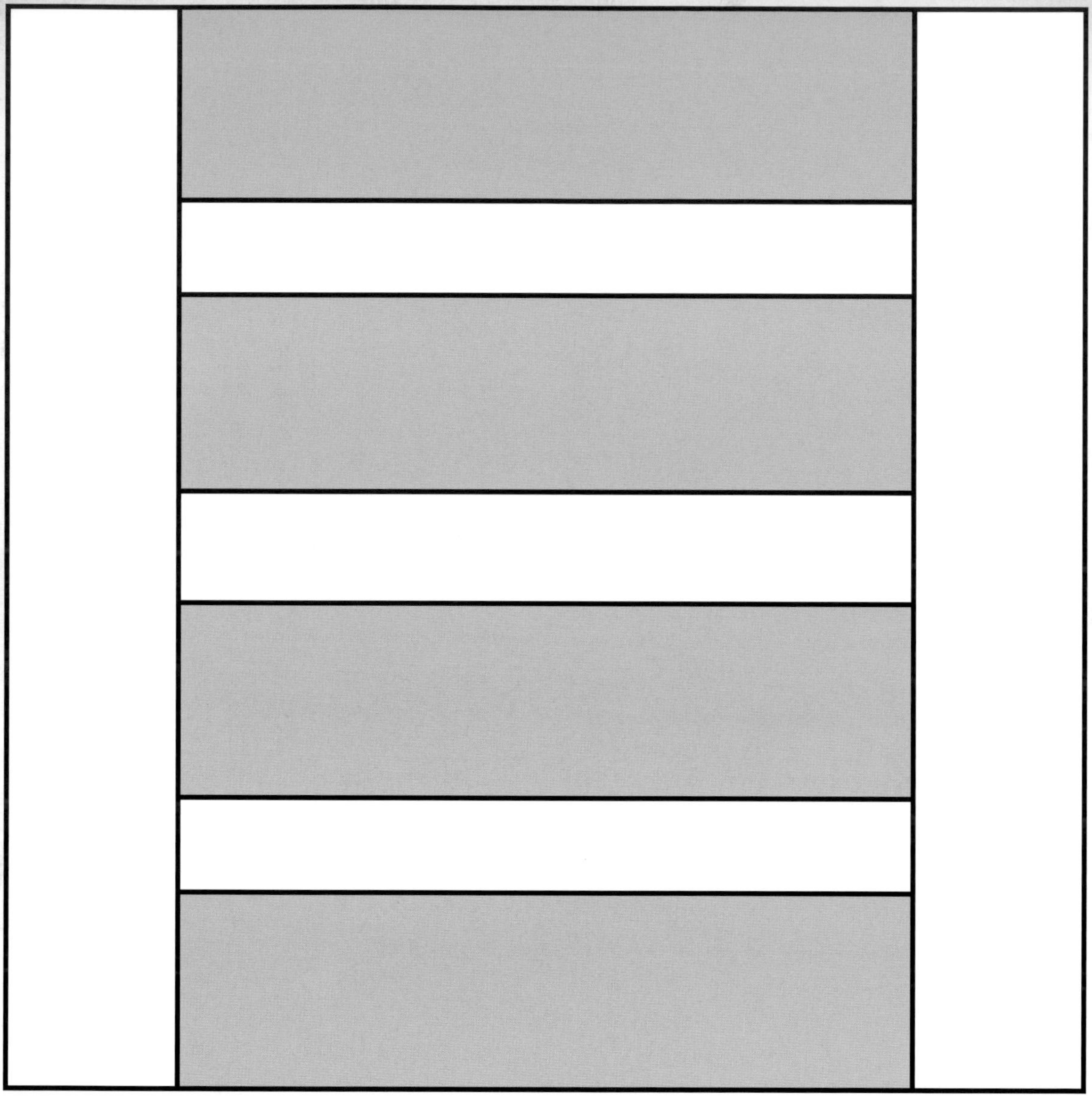

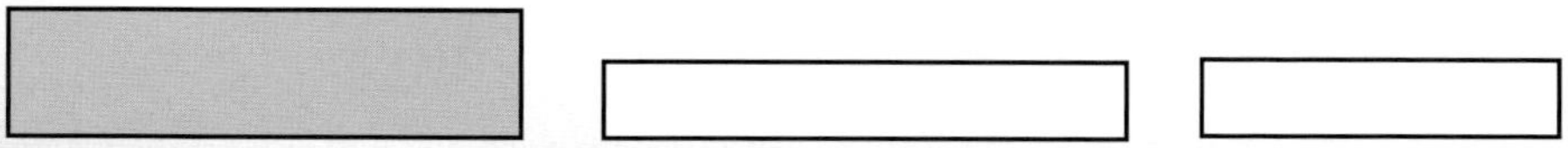

1⅝" × 4½" (4)

1" × 6½" (2)

1" × 4½" (3)

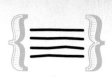

Tramps, as we called them, were a common sight in our town, a suburb of San Francisco. They walked the streets looking for an X mark in front of a house (the signal to all they could get food here). Our house always had an X in front, either on the first cement step or on the curb. My mother never turned a man away.

The tramps used to ring the doorbell and say that they were hungry but willing to do any odd job for a meal or some food. Sometimes mother would let them do a little garden work and when she had no odd job they would ask to use her broom, saying the least they could do is sweep the porch and sidewalk for her.

— GENEVIEVE WOODS,
California

Enid, Oklahoma, was a little mid-western town then. When the train stopped I hopped out of the boxcar along with my buddy. We were both hungry, so we headed for town, but in different directions. There are times when two can be a crowd.

I walked through and beyond the center of town and began to see many large, but rather dilapidated, homes. Behind or beside these homes there were always large gardens. And this was a good sign. Especially in August. People with large gardens and lawns always had odd jobs for a man to do. I turned in at one friendly-looking house. Through the screen door I saw a woman moving about. This was good. Usually a woman was more sympathetic toward a hungry wanderer.

I went up the steps and knocked on the kitchen door. The woman looked up, startled, and said, "Yes?" She came to the door.

"Ma'am, would you have any odd jobs a man could do for a meal?"

"Odd jobs, is it? And what kind of odd jobs can you do?"

"I can do anything."

"Let me see your hands," she said. This was a common procedure. The police often used it. It was a means of separating the sheep from the goats; that is, the hobos from the bums. If your hands were pink and smooth, obviously you were a bum and never worked. If your hands were rough and calloused, you were a hobo. Hobos were workers, often good workers. But they were restless; just couldn't stay in one place; couldn't settle down. The woman was apparently satisfied. "Let's see how good you are at digging up potatoes." She handed me a garden fork and an empty bushel basket.

"All right, go to it," she said.

An hour later, when I had filled the basket with fresh, new potatoes, Mrs. Svenson (that was her name) came back out, and was pleased to see what I had done. "Good job, boy," she said, and took me into the kitchen to the biggest and best meal I'd had in weeks. Plus a couple of sandwiches for "the road."

 RALPH SHELLY,
Ohio

Photograph by Dorothea Lange, Courtesy of the Library of Congress, lc-usf347-003801-ze

1⅜" × 6½" (3)　　　　　1⅜" × 1⅜" (12)　1⅜" × 1⅜" (16)

{#} JAIL

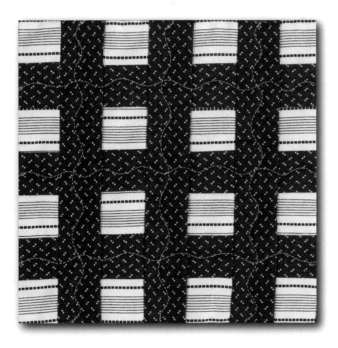

The hobos said, "You cannot ride passenger trains. The bulls will grab you and throw you in jail." I was desperate to get home, so I grabbed on the back of the engine, and the electrified passenger train pulled away from the Seattle Union Station. The rain came in torrents all night long, as I stood on the back of the engine. The next morning, after we stopped in Butte, Montana, the engineer said to me, "For God's sake boy, it's a miracle that you weren't electrocuted last night!"

— PAUL BOOKER,
California

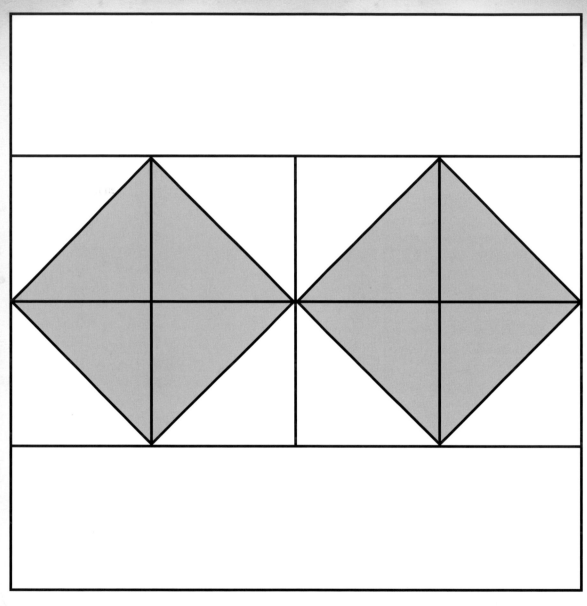

2" × 6½" (2)   2⅜" (8)   2⅜" (8)

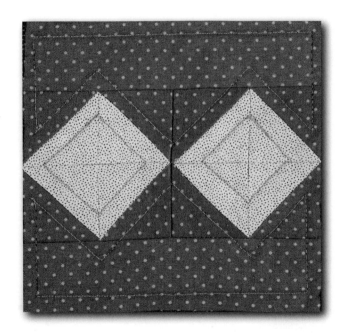

One of my older brothers fell from a train in Iowa. Lost a leg and a short time later his life in 1919 or 1920. I fell from a train at Wreath, Oregon, and was knocked unconscious for some time. I never road another freight.

— GEORGE F. PHILLIPS,
Missouri

Appliqué
If desired, use embroidery floss to add whiskers to the cat's face.

KIND-HEARTED LADY

I can remember one cold, snowy, below-zero day, when a hobo came to the back door. Mother had just heated up some tomato soup to go with our sandwiches, so she grabbed up a bowl and filled it with soup, then proceeded to tell the hobo to step inside the door to drink the soup and warm up a bit. He refused to do so, and we all felt so badly because he looked half frozen. He stood just outside the back door, spooned up the soup and ate the sandwich Mother gave him, then, as he left the empty bowl on the kitchen floor, he quietly said, "May God always bless you, Madam." Mom had tears in her eyes as she watched him walk down the back alley to the railroad tracks.

— Patricia P. Schreiner,
Michigan

109

Appliqué

{☒} MAN WITH A GUN

Four men and I were in a "reefer" coming into the railroad yards of Longview, Texas when we heard loud gunfire! "My God," one man said, "that must be Texas Slim" (a railroad detective that was meaner than a rattlesnake). We scurried out of the empty ice compartment to the top of the boxcar, and a few cars down, there was the dreaded Texas Slim shouting, "I'll kill every one of you!" We fled for our lives, as this demon from hell fired wildly at us.

— PAUL BOOKER,
California

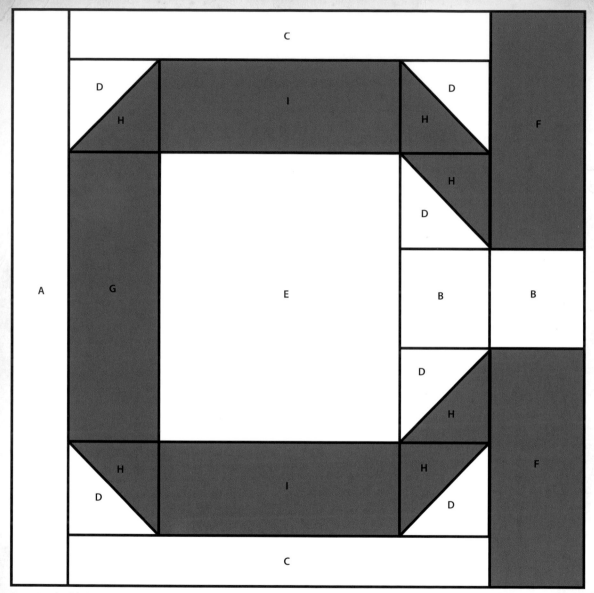

Reversing this block reverses this meaning: Rotate the block 180 degrees for the sign "Owner Home."

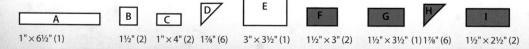

A
1" × 6½" (1)

B
1½" (2)

C
1" × 4" (2)

D
1⅞" (6)

E
3" × 3½" (1)

F
1½" × 3" (2)

G
1½" × 3½" (1)

H
1⅞" (6)

I
1½" × 2½" (2)

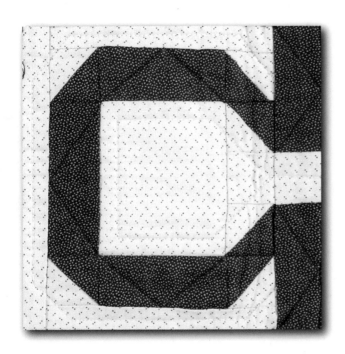

I was sitting on a railroad track, somewhere in Montana, waiting for a freight train. I was nineteen years old. It was getting dark, and as I looked down at a village below I saw a Christmas tree lit up in a window and children playing around it. That was the first I knew it was Christmas. Tears ran down my cheeks as I remembered Christmas day when I was the age of those children.

— DONALD E. NEWHOUSER,
Indiana

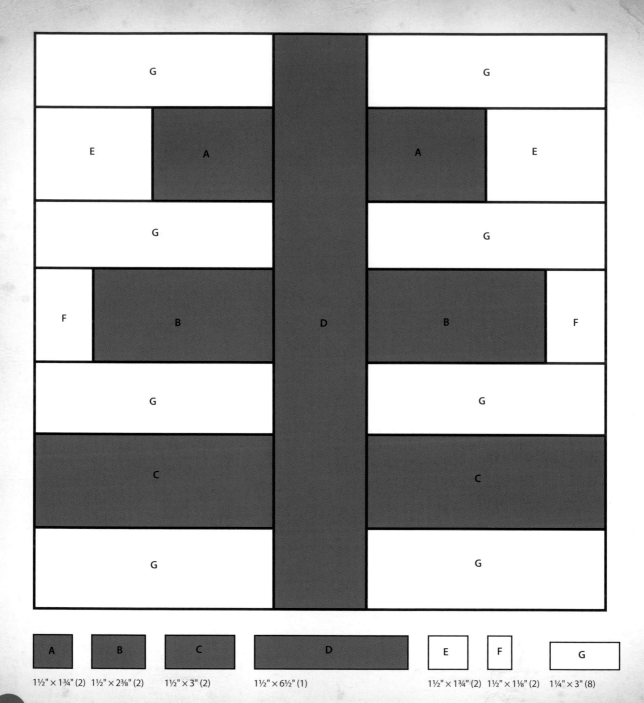

A	B	C	D	E	F	G
1½" × 1¾" (2)	1½" × 2⅜" (2)	1½" × 3" (2)	1½" × 6½" (1)	1½" × 1¾" (2)	1½" × 1⅛" (2)	1¼" × 3" (8)

We never ventured into the South for we heard stories about chain gangs and the cruel treatment of those caught. I found it worthwhile to stay clean and try to dress as well as possible and people were more apt to help. Most Western towns would allow you to sleep overnight in their jails and many would give you day-old rolls and coffee the next morning. Once a town marshal brought us home with him and put us on a mattress in his basement. I have always felt guilty for we were hungry and each ate a quart of his canned peaches. Another one put us in a hotel and gave us a chit for breakfast the next morning.

— BUD HUGHES,
Nebraska

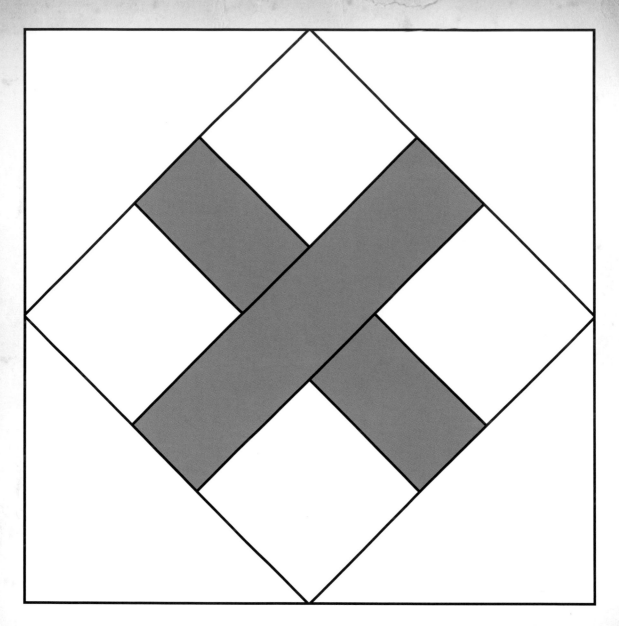

 3⅞" (4)   2⅛" (4)   1½" × 2⅛" (2)   4¾" × 1½" (1)

{✕} OK

I learned that there are all kinds of people in the world, and that you never know what tomorrow is going to bring, and that things don't always turn out like you wish they would. And when you get thrown off, just get up and give it another shot. And learn that the world doesn't just exist for you. All in all I have had a pretty good life.

— CHARLES RANKIN,
Ohio

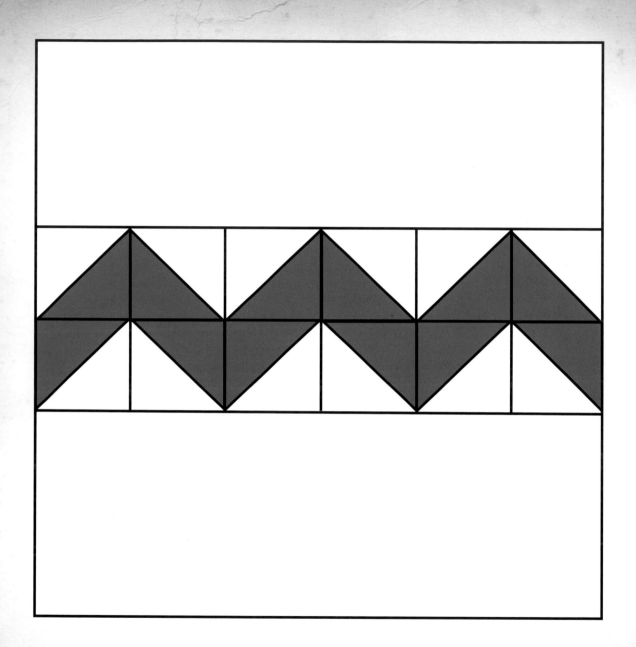

1⅞" (8) 1⅞" (8) 2½" × 6½" (2)

I had $3.50 when I left from Vancover, Washington on the SP&S Line up the Columbia River to Spokane. I bought some food and in some division towns I was able to get food chits worth fifteen to twenty cents. I ran out of money in Milwaukee and did not eat for the last three days except for a large onion that I took from a boxcar and which I was taking home to show as it was the biggest onion that I had ever seen, but hunger prevailed.

— HAROLD SPARKS,
Virginia

I was one of five children. My father was an out-of-work iron worker, until FDR set up where the men could work two or three days a week. We lived in a company-owned, three-room house with the bath room on the tiny back porch. I married when I had just finished the 7th grade, so my parents would have one less mouth to feed. Myself, my two sisters and my mother all wore a size eight to ten dress and a size five shoe. So one of us got to wear it one Sunday, then it would pass on to the next sister and so on. Daddy and Mother fed the seven of us on $7.00 per week. Only one time did we go hungry. Daddy and the other men in our neighborhood would take toe sacks and go down the railroad track and pick up spilled coal to heat the stove in the kitchen and the fireplace in the front room. I couldn't help but wonder, when Daddy would come home with coal dust all over his clothes and in his hair if he picked it up on the track or had he climbed down inside the coal car? I came home for lunch each day from school and Mother would send me to the store to buy the food for our supper. No one ever even mentioned lunch. Except on Saturday we all shared a total of a half gallon of home-canned peaches. But Sunday was the big day. A chicken (one) and dumplings was our regular Sunday dinner—Big Day.

Jo Lamb Fulton,
Tennessee

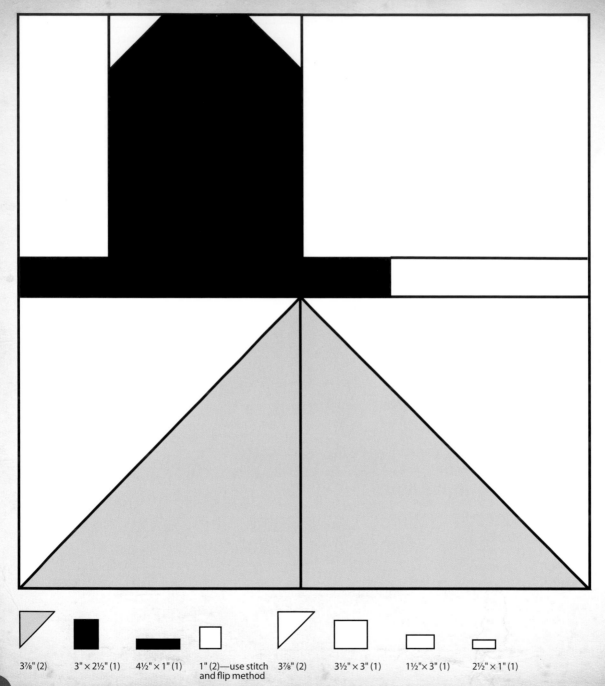

3⅞" (2)   3" × 2½" (1)   4½" × 1" (1)   1" (2)—use stitch and flip method   3⅞" (2)   3½" × 3" (1)   1½" × 3" (1)   2½" × 1" (1)

I was down to three cents in Gallop, New Mexico heading for Los Angeles. A buddy of mine and I were walking along Highway 66 when I saw a sows ear purse on the shoulder of the road. It had no ID and no one showed up to claim it. It had a little over $12.00 in coins. The best meal we had in weeks.

H.B. "Down the Road Doc" Harmon,
California

123

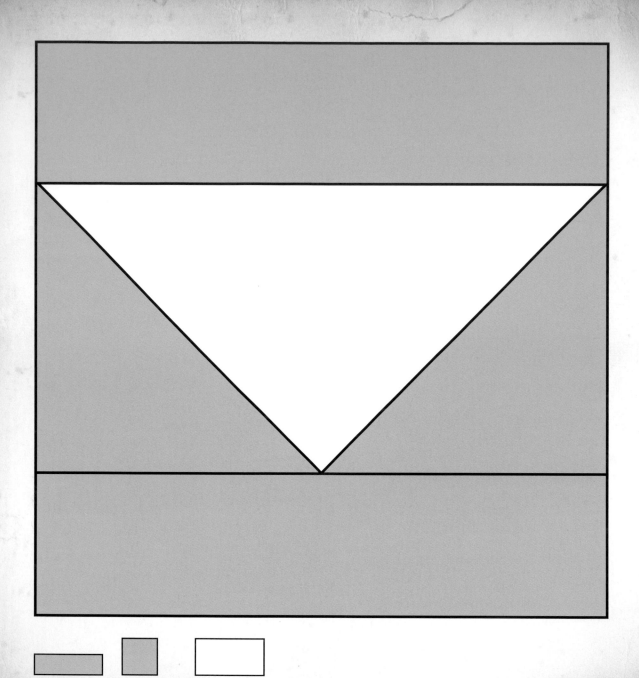

2" × 6½" (2)

3½" (2)—use
stitch and flip
method

3½" × 6½" (1)

I remember a hobo jungle with 1800 hobos at Phoenix, Arizona. That was the day that FDR got elected … He was the best of them all.

— BEN CRUMP,
California

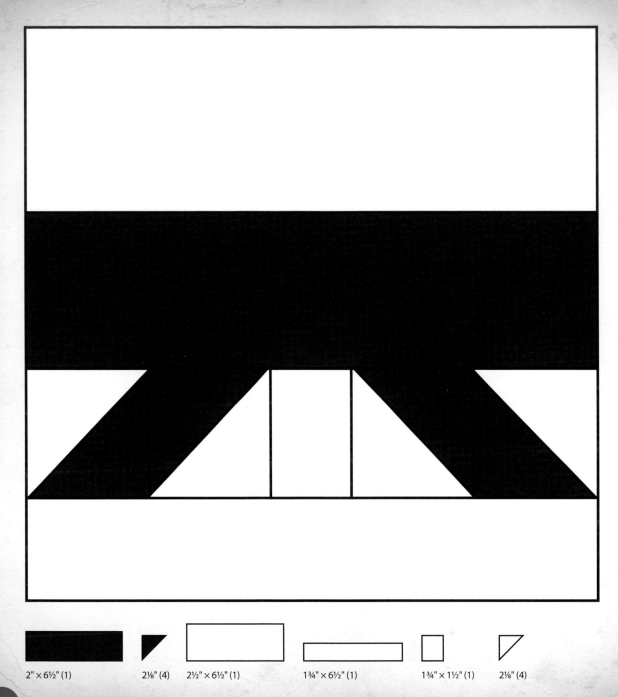

2" × 6½" (1)   2⅛" (4)   2½" × 6½" (1)   1¾" × 6½" (1)   1¾" × 1½" (1)   2⅛" (4)

{⌐} SIT-DOWN FEED

The most impressive sight I saw was a fully loaded freight train winding through the mountains of the southwest with several hundred people on the tops and sides of the cars.

— ARTHUR HUNEVEN,
California

 2⅜" (8)   3½" (1)   3½" × 1½" (1)   3½" × 1½" (2)   2⅜" (8) 1¾" (4)—use stitch and flip method

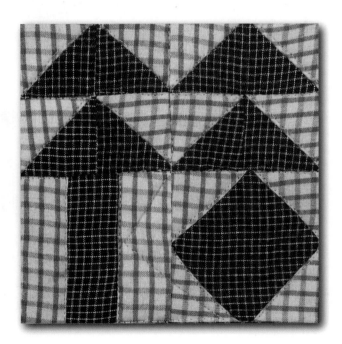

I t was back in 1937. I was just fifteen years old at the time. I was born in 1922 on a farm in Saginaw County, Michigan and me and another boy same age hopped a freight train. I guess we got a little tired of working on the farm every day. The railroad tracks ran right next to our property and every time we seen a train go by we'd go to the tracks to watch and were amazed at all the hobos that rode the train. I guess in a way it looked like a fun thing to do, that is until you run out of money. We only had $15.00 between us. It was during the month of July, but the nights were still cold sleeping on those hard wooden floors in the boxcars if you were lucky. But we even slept in fields under hay stacks to keep warm.

We headed for Chicago, then caught another train for out west. And whenever the train stopped we tried to get a little to eat, mostly bananas or just franks or a loaf of bread and water. Lots of time we had to catch the train on the run account of the railroad dicks. And one time we had to jump off of one. It just happened to be on a sandy curve and they usually slow down on a curve. Yet we tumbled in the sand for about fifty feet. But when we ran out of money we turned around and headed for

(Continued on next page.)

home. We were somewhere in Iowa. We decided to catch the first train we seen going east and caught one in the middle of the night. The last day we didn't have anything to eat. And to make matters worse, my buddy caught the train and I didn't make it. It was going too fast. So I decide to hitchhike the rest of the way home. I didn't have a penny to my name and it was hot, about ninety degrees on that highway, thirsty and hungry. But finally I got a ride from nice old gentleman that was going right to my home town. And I think after that experience I was glad to be working back on the farm and just watch the trains go by. But it just happens that my story had a Paul Harvey ending. And here is the rest of the story. After riding for a while with this elderly man he was going to stop and get a bite to eat, and asked if I wanted to eat too. I told him I was hungry enough to eat, but I haven't a cent on me. So he said "Come on. I'll buy you your meal." So after riding the rest of the way home I thanked him for the ride and the meal. I said, "I sure hope I could do something for him some day." Well, our paths cross again 10 years later. I spent 4 more years on the farm, then got into the Navy until after World War II. Then got married and bought a home and he was an insurance salesman. So I bought all my insurance from him and he became a good friend until his death. But I'll always remember this kind old man who was so good to a young boy, and always be grateful just for knowing him.

EDWARD REXIUS,
Michigan

PHOTOGRAPH BY J. DOODY, COURTESY OF THE LIBRARY OF CONGRESS, LC-USZ62-120293

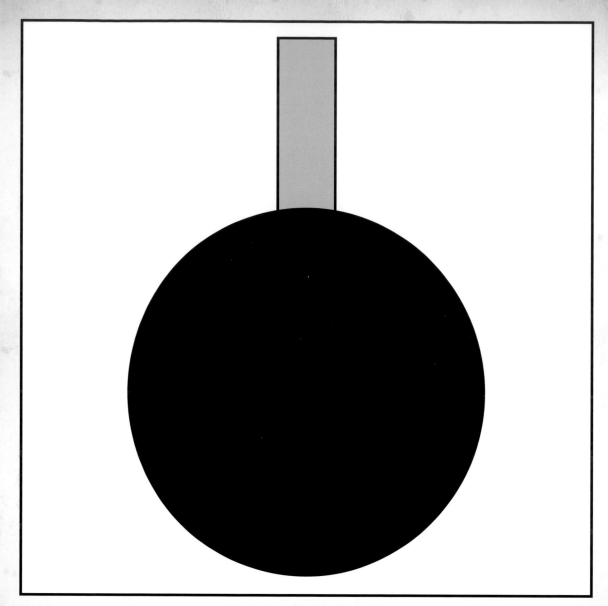

Appliqué

{ } STRAIGHT AHEAD

In those days many of my friends were heading for California. All you needed was an old car that would run, a five gallon can and an "Oklahoma credit card" (about 4 feet of garden hose). You would be out of gas along the road (all gravel), and someone would stop and let you siphon a couple of gallons from their gas tank. At the next town there was usually a place to wash dishes or something for some grub.

— LARRY KUEBEL,
Nebraska

 3½" × 2" (1)   6½" × 2" (1)   2" (1)   2¾" × 2" (2)   2¾" × 3½" (2)

We went on to the next house, and knocked on the door. A lady came to the door, and we asked her for something to eat also. She said, "Wait a minute." She was gone several minutes and finally came to the door and handed us two very dry slices of bread. She said, "Now, boys I'm not giving you this for your sakes, or my sake, but I'm giving it to you for the Lord's sake." Lyle took the bread and forlorn-looking in his way said, "Lady, please for God's sake, would you go back and put a little butter or jam on it ... huh?"

ULAN S. MILLER,
Missouri

Appliqué

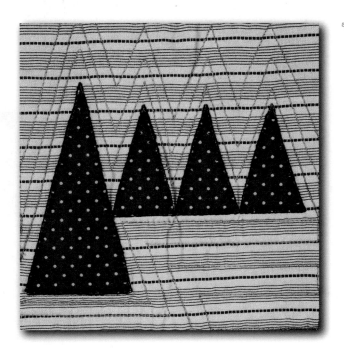

When I was riding through Texas a baby was born to a young girl in a boxcar that I happened to be in. A much older man, grandfather, probably, was with her. There were three others besides myself riding along with them. An old bindle stiff offered a clean white sock to tie around the baby's middle. Named the baby Toyah, after the town that the train would be stopping at next and there were taken away by ambulance, remember that they wouldn't let the old man ride with them. Often I have wondered where he might be today (the baby)!

— BILLY A. WATKINS,
Indiana

137

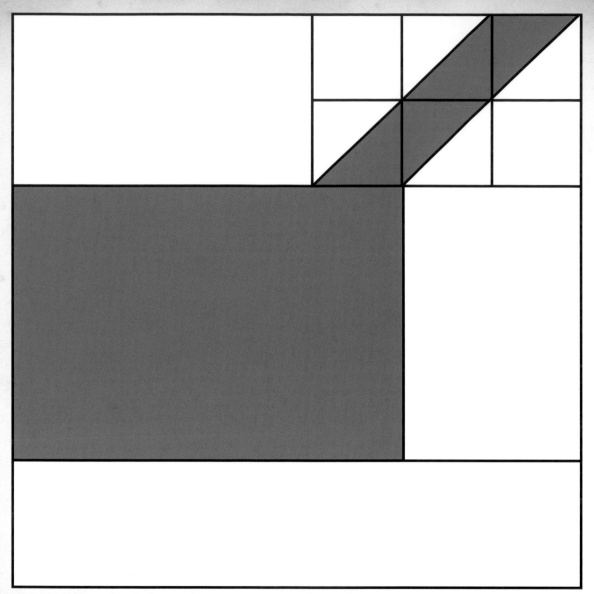

Reversing this block reverses this meaning: Rotate the block 180 degrees for the sign "Town Does Not Allow Alcohol."

1⅞" (4)   3½" × 4½" (1)   1⅞" (4)   1½" (2)   1½" × 6½" (1)   2½" × 3½" (2)

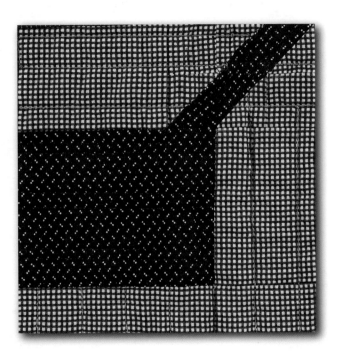
There were over a million hobos on the road during that time drifting from place to place. In some cases there were whole families riding in the same boxcar. There was a real mixture of people and each day and each mile was an education you could never get anywhere else. It was an adventure you could not duplicate in today's culture and environment. There was danger involved and I saw young and old men shot, stabbed, robbed and beaten, killed in accidents and also murdered by others for a handful of coins. There was much drinking of potent and lethal liquids even back then.

— STEPHEN A. TOMKO,
Pennsylvania

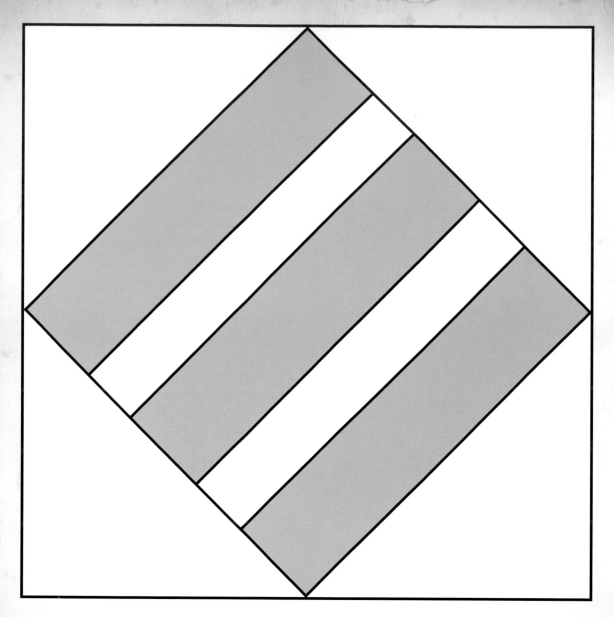

3⅞" (4)   1½" × 4¾" (3)   1⅛" × 4¾" (2)

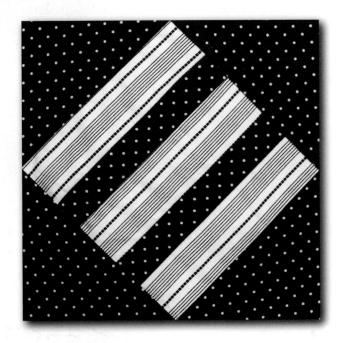

We knew from experience that the railroad bulls were always looking for hitchhikers like us, and we also wanted to stay clear of the hobo camps. The 'bos in these camps were professional riders; mean and tough who were not to be trusted.

— VICTOR MARTENS,
Indiana

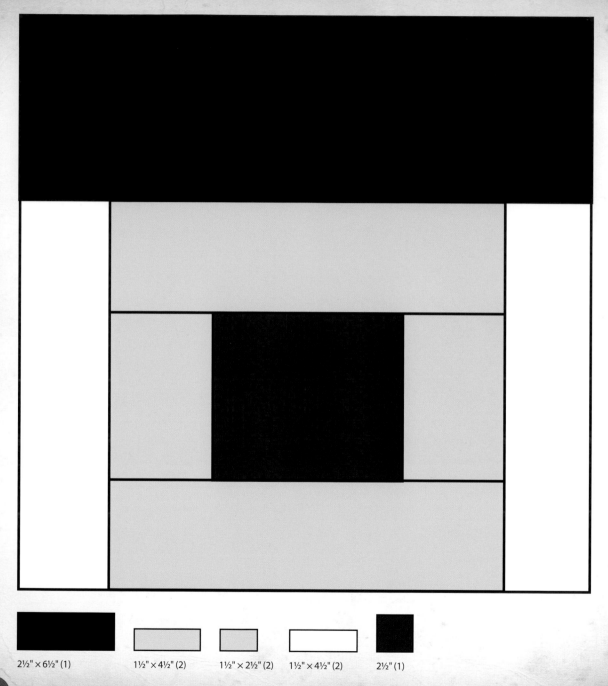

2½" × 6½" (1)   1½" × 4½" (2)   1½" × 2½" (2)   1½" × 4½" (2)   2½" (1)

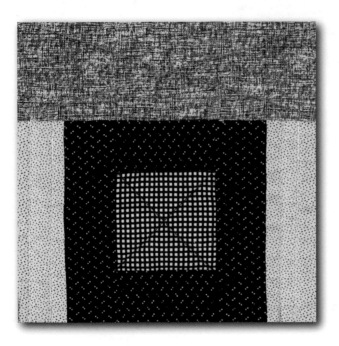

WELL-GUARDED HOUSE

During the early years of the great depression (1930–1936) I was of high school age, living at home with my parents and siblings. My father was a railroad engineer on the Erie Railroad but was still firing coal-burning locomotives. Our hometown was Port Jervis, New York, just ninety miles northwest of New York City.

On many occasions Dad would hide out hobos in the coal tender behind the engine, and mother usually had an extra sandwich and piece of cake tucked away in the lunch pail to feed a hungry man. Dad knew where the bulls hung out and would inform the 'bos where to leave the train and where to rejoin another.

JOHN McKINNEY, JR.,
Nebraska

Appliqué

{ } WOMAN

Once a man came to the door asking for food. "Come in. Come in." He stood there a moment, then said, "But I have a family with me." "Bring them, bring them." They came, a wife and three children. But they wouldn't come into the house. "We would eat outside, on the ground." So Mother spread some homemade rugs on the ground and they ate: homemade bread and baked beans. He couldn't thank us enough.

— ANN WALKO,
Pennsylvania

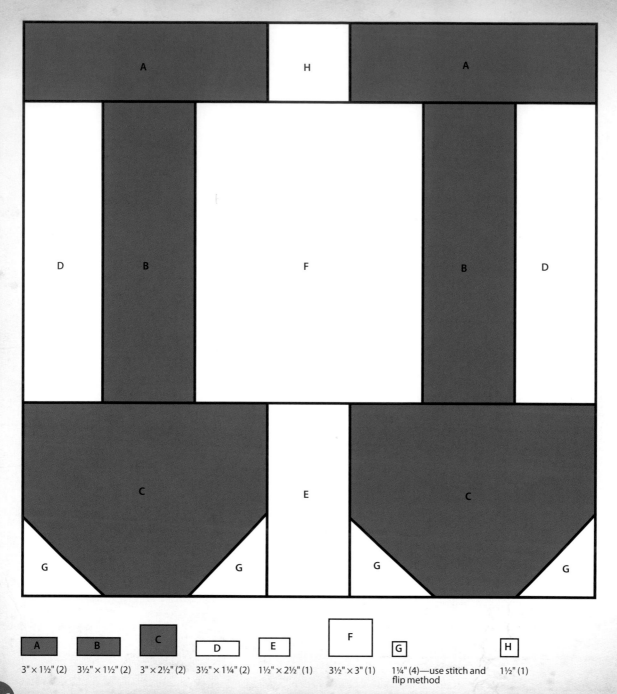

A
3" × 1½" (2)

B
3½" × 1½" (2)

C
3" × 2½" (2)

D
3½" × 1¼" (2)

E
1½" × 2½" (1)

F
3½" × 3" (1)

G
1¼" (4)—use stitch and flip method

H
1½" (1)

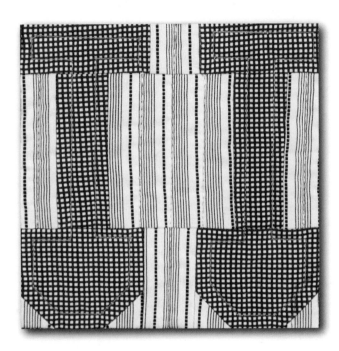

After working as a bundle handler for a thrashing rig near Minot, North Dakota, I still did not have enough money to pay my tuition to the University of North Dakota. To get to Minot I had hitchhiked and was picked up by a fellow from Kansas driving a Model A Ford with a rumble seat. He and two fellows from Iowa had worked with me on the threshing crew. They were going to Washington to pick apples. If I would put my money in the pot, they would take me to Washington.

In Washington near Wenatche, we thinned pears, picked pears, thinned Delicious apples, then picked apples. I earned enough money to pay my tuition and sent it back to North Dakota.

I then found a neighbor who could tell me something of the tricks of riding the rails. He said a brakeman would usually tell me what train was going the direction I wanted to go and the approximate time of departure. He told me that I could tell when the train was ready to leave when the engineer gave the "high ball," two short toots.

— MORRIS B. THOMTE,
Montana

147

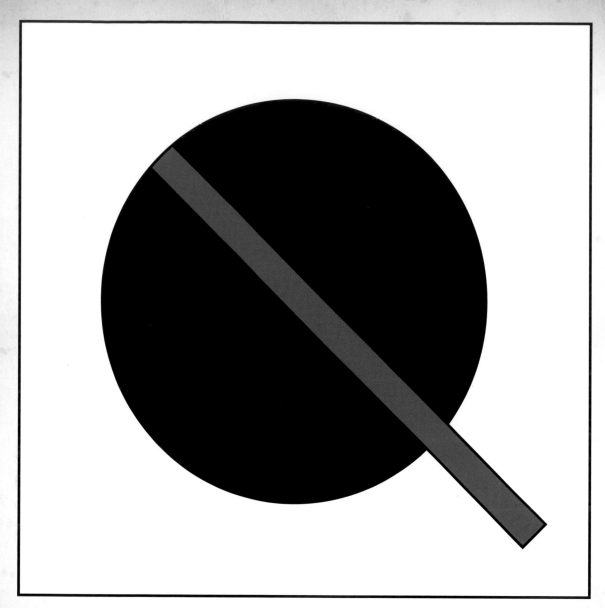

Appliqué

I have one memory of a hobo standing outside the screen door, and Mother handing food out the door to him. I don't believe she ever denied any of them something to eat; a hunk of cornbread or something.

I do recall that she got real mad once. Seems she had left clothes hanging out on the line out on the hill, and some of Daddy's long johns and other clothing disappeared, and also something (perhaps bacon) out of the smoke house. I remember she was real mad! Said she wasn't going to give out any more food, but I am sure she did not hold to that. The hobos traveling through that poor area sure must have had our place marked real good. The hobos never went to that mean Lou's house next door to ask for anything!

— BETTY M. GLOVER,
Virginia

149

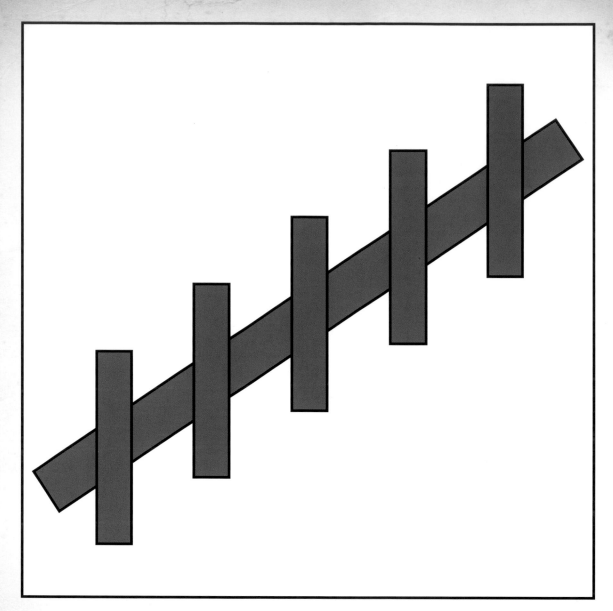

Appliqué

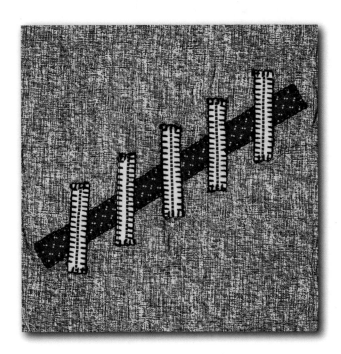

One day it was pretty and warm and I was starved so I walked up a driveway and knocked on the back door to my left. When the lady came to the door I asked for work to get something to eat. She said she didn't feed tramps and I said, "Lady, I'm not a tramp. I am a hobo."

"What the hell is the difference?" she asked.

"Well," I told her, "A tramp won't work and a hobo will."

"Well, I don't feed hobos either," she said, and slammed the door.

I thanked her for her time and walked across the driveway. The back doors faced each other. I knocked on the other door and a lady came to the door and I asked her what I had asked the other lady. She said she didn't have any work but I looked hungry so have a seat on the steps. I did and in a few minutes she had a nice plate of food and a big glass of iced tea for me. I was really enjoying the food when the grouch next door stuck her head out the screen door and asked if I could eat some mashed potatoes. I said, "Yes ma'am." Here she comes with a nice plate of food. I guess she was ashamed of the way she had acted but I left that driveway full as a tick and happy as a lark.

— JAMES PEARSON,
New York

Projects

154

MULLIGAN STEW

Mulligan Stew was always a welcome meal for the travel-weary hobo. My quilt version of Mulligan Stew is almost all of the blocks mixed together. I think it looks pretty tasty! Your Stew can use any variety of blocks. These measurements are based on 6" finished blocks.

Materials List
for 41" × 41" Wall Quilt

20 Hobo Blocks of your choice pieced from scrap fabric
Sashing: ¼ yard
Inner Border: ¼ yard
Outer Border: ⅞ yard
Binding: ½ yard
Backing: 2½ yards
Batting: 48" × 48"

Cutting List
for 41" × 41" Wall Quilt

Cut 5 strips 1½" × WOF for Sashing, then from these strips cut the following:
  3 strips 1½" × 27½"
  12 strips 1½" × 6½"

Cut 4 strips 1½" × WOF for Inner Border, then from these strips cut the following:
  2 strips 1½" × 27½"
  2 strips 1½" × 29½"

Cut 4 strips 6½" × WOF for Outer Border, then from these strips cut the following:
  4 strips 6½" × 29½"

Materials List
for 62" × 69" Lap Quilt

60 Hobo Blocks of your choice pieced from scrap fabric
Sashing: 1 yard
Inner Border: ⅓ yard
Outer Border: 1⅜ yards
Binding: ⅔ yard
Backing: 4 yards
Batting: 70" × 80"

Cutting List
for 62" × 69" Lap Quilt

Cut 9 strips 1½" × WOF for Sashing, then from these strips cut the following:
  49 strips 1½" × 6½"

Cut 9 strips 1½" × WOF for Sashing, sew together into one strip, then from this strip cut the following:
  6 strips 1½" × 55½"

Cut 6 strips 1½" × WOF for Inner Border, sew together into one strip, then from this strip cut the following:
  2 strips 1½" × 50½"
  2 strips 1½" × 55½"

Cut 7 strips 6½" × WOF for Outer Border, sew together into one strip, then from this strip cut the following:
  2 strips 6½" × 50½"
  2 strips 6½" × 57½"

Materials List
for 83" × 97" Full Quilt

124 Hobo Blocks of your choice pieced from scrap fabric
Sashing: 1¾ yards
Inner Border: ⅜ yard
Outer Border: 1¾ yards
Binding: ¾ yard
Backing: 7½ yards
Batting: 90" × 107"

Cutting List
for 83" × 97" Full Quilt

Cut 20 strips 1½" × WOF for Sashing, then from these strips cut the following:
  120 strips 1½" × 6½"

Cut 18 strips 1½" × WOF for Sashing, sew together into one strip, then from this strip cut the following:
  9 strips 1½" × 83½"

Cut 8 strips 1½" × WOF for Inner Border, sew together into one strip, then from this strip cut the following:
  2 strips 1½" × 71½"
  2 strips 1½" × 83½"

Cut 8 strips 6½" × WOF for Outer Border, sew together into one strip, then from this strip cut the following:
  2 strips 6½" × 71½"
  2 strips 6½" × 85½"

Designed by Debra Henninger, Pieced and Appliquéd by Debra Henninger and Sharon Janzen, Quilted by Jeri Rennie

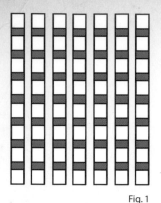

Fig. 1

Assembly Instructions

▷ Lay out the blocks in rows: 4 × 4 for the Wall Quilt, 7 × 8 for the Lap Quilt and 10 × 12 for the Full Quilt. Arrange the hobo blocks as desired. You will have 4 blocks left to be used as cornerstones.

▷ Sew a 6½" sashing strip to the bottom of each of the blocks except for the blocks in the bottom row.

▷ Sew the blocks into columns (Fig. 1).

▷ Sew a long sashing strip to the right-hand side of each column except the far right column.

▷ Sew the columns into sets of twos, then those sets in twos, and so forth until all of the columns are sewn together (Fig 2).

▷ Sew the shorter inner border strips to the top and bottom of the quilt.

▷ Sew the remaining inner border strips to the sides of the quilt (Fig. 3).

▷ Sew the shorter outer border strips to the top and bottom of the quilt.

▷ Sew the remaining hobo blocks to each end of the two longer border strips and sew these strips to the sides of the quilt (Fig. 4).

▷ Quilt. Bind. Enjoy!

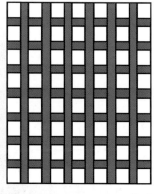

Fig. 2

Illustrations are for the 62" × 69" Lap Quilt

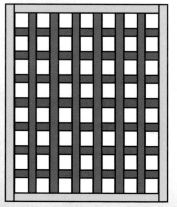

Fig. 3

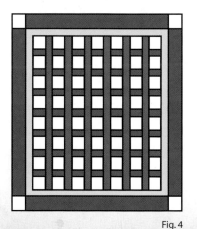

Fig. 4

These constant travelers gathered in places called jungles. These were usually located on railroad land or on marginal land such as swamps or barren, open areas. It should be close to some water. This was necessary for cooking and on rare occasions necessary for bathing. The jungle would be strewn with fire-blackened tin cans. There were some flat pieces of iron used as a crude stovetop. There were many fire pits usually ringed with rocks. This was an eating and sleeping place. Some distance away, and hopefully downwind, was the toilet ground.

RALPH H. SHIRLEY,
Montana

RIDIN' THE RAILS

Trains were a vital mode of transportation to a penniless population looking for work, a new life, warm weather or even just an adventure. Even though riding the rails was dangerous and difficult, it conjures up romantic images of a kind of freedom most of us can only dream of.

Materials List
for 79" × 89" Full Quilt

15 Hobo Blocks of your choice
Sashing: ⅞ yard
Inner Border: ⅝ yard
Track Border: 1¼ yards
Corner Stones: ⅓ yard
Outer Border: 1¾ yards
Binding: ⅔ yard
Backing: 7¼ yards
Batting: 90" × 100"

Materials List
for 97" × 102" Queen Quilt

24 Hobo Blocks of your choice
Sashing: 1 yard
Inner Border: ⅝ yard
Track Border: 1¼ yards
Corner Stones: ⅓ yard
Outer Border: 2½ yards
Binding: ⅞ yard
Backing: 8¾ yards
Batting: 107" × 112"

Materials List for Blocks
(same for both sizes)

Background: ¼ yard (per block)
Darks: 1/16 yard (per block—for wheels and undercarriage)
Mediums: ¼ yard (per block)

☞ *Note: This yardage is enough to make the blocks, Engine, Caboose and Boxcars. However, I think scraps are the way to go!*

Cutting List
for 79" × 89" Full Quilt

Cut 13 strips 1½" × WOF for Sashing, sew together into one strip, then from this strip cut the following:
      6 strips 1½" × 54½"
      2 strips 1½" × 66½"

Cut 7 strips 2" × WOF for Inner Border, sew together into one strip, then from this strip cut the following:
      2 strips 2" × 56½"
      2 strips 2" × 69½"

Cut 8 strips 4½" × WOF for Track Border, sew together into one strip, then from this strip cut the following:
      2 strips 4½" × 59½"
      2 strips 4½" × 69½"

Cut 4 squares 4½" for Corner Stones

Cut 13 strips 6½" × WOF for Outer Border, sew together into one strip, then from this strip cut the following:
      2 strips 6½" × 67½"
      2 strips 6½" × 89½"

Cutting List
for 97" × 102" Queen Quilt

Cut 18 strips 1½" × WOF for Sashing, sew together into one strip, then from this strip cut the following:
      7 strips 1½" × 72½"
      2 strips 1½" × 79½"

Cut 9 strips 2" × WOF for Inner Border, sew together into one strip, then from this strip cut the following:
      2 strips 2" × 74½"
      2 strips 2" × 82½"

Cut 9 strips 4½" × WOF for Track Border, sew together into one strip, then from this strip cut the following:
      2 strips 4½" × 77½"
      2 strips 4½" × 82½"

Cut 4 squares 4½" for Corner Stones

Cut 9 strips 6½" × WOF for Outer Border, sew together into one strip, then from this strip cut the following:
      2 strips 6½" × 85½"
      2 strips 6½" × 102½"

{ HELPFUL HINT }

The Track Border fabric needs to be a stripe (cut perpendicular to the stripe). Because it is a stripe, I suggest you sew the strips together with a straight seam rather than with the normal diagonal seam to maintain the stripe pattern.

DESIGNED BY DEBRA HENNINGER, PIECED AND APPLIQUÉD BY SHARON JANZEN, QUILTED BY JERI RENNIE

Assembly Instructions

▷ Create an Engine block using the Engine pattern on page 162.

▷ Create a Caboose using the Caboose pattern on page 164.

▷ Create a Boxcar for each of the remaining blocks using the Boxcar pattern on page 163.

▷ Create the Tracks with the track border fabric. Mark each strip 1½" from each edge lengthwise (Fig. 1), then place black bias tape down the center of each mark, and sew each edge of the bias tape down. I highly recommend using a fusible bias tape. Also, sewing the bias tape down with a twin needle will make the job much easier and you will be more pleased with the finished look.

▷ Lay the blocks out in rows: 3 × 5 for the Full Quilt, 4 × 6 for the Queen Quilt. Place the engine in the top left corner and the caboose in the bottom right corner (Fig. 2).

▷ Sew the blocks together into rows.

▷ Sew a shorter sashing strip to the top and bottom of the top row, and to the bottom of each of the remaining rows.

▷ Sew the rows together.

▷ Sew the longer sashing strips to each side of the quilt.

▷ Sew the shorter inner border strips to the top and bottom of the quilt.

▷ Sew the longer inner border strips to the sides of the quilt.

▷ Sew a shorter track border strip to the top and bottom of the quilt.

▷ Sew the cornerstone blocks to each end of the longer track border strips; sew the strips and cornerstones to the sides of the quilt.

▷ Sew the shorter outer border strips to the top and bottom of the quilt.

▷ Sew the longer outer border strips to the sides of the quilt.

▷ Quilt. Bind. Enjoy!

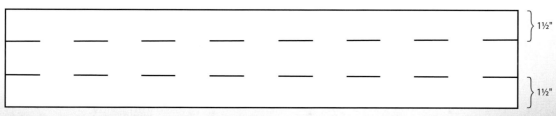

1½"

1½"

Fig. 1

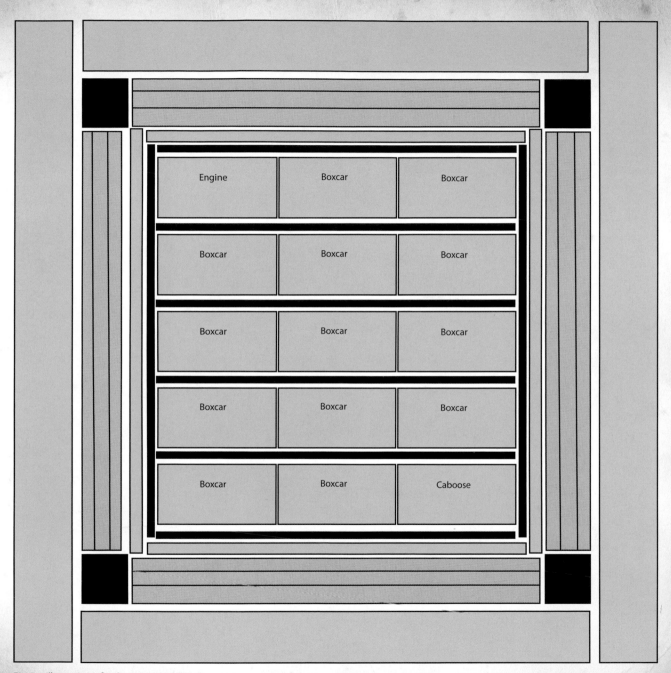

Fig. 2   Illustration is for the 79" × 89" Full Quilt

Engine (18½" × 12½" unfinished)

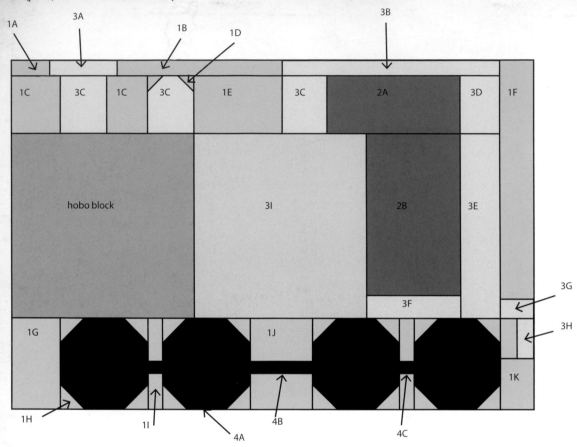

1A: 1" × 1½" (1)
1B: 1" × 6" (1)
1C: 2½" × 2" (2)
1D: ¾" × ¾"
(2)—use stitch and
flip method

1E: 2½" × 2½" (1)
1F: 8½" × 1½" (1)
1G: 4" × 1½" (1)
1H: 1½" × 1½"
(16)—use stitch
and flip method

1I: 2" × 1" (5)
1J: 2" × 1½" (2)
1K: 2½" × 1½" (1)
2A: 2½" × 6" (1)
2B: 5" × 3½" (1)
3A: 1" × 3" (1)

3B: 1" × 8½" (1)
3C: 2½" × 2" (3)
3D: 2½" × 2½" (1)
3E: 6½" × 2½" (1)
3F: 1" × 3½" (1)
3G: 1" × 1½" (1)

3H: 2" × 1" (1)
3I: 6½" × 6½" (1)
4A: 4" × 4" (4)
4B: 1" × 1½" (1)
4C: 1" × 1" (2)

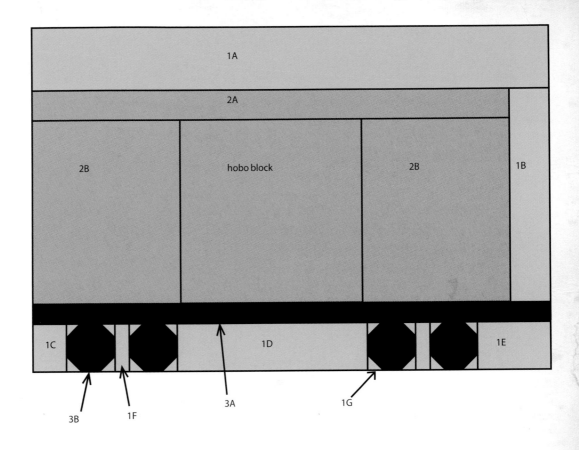

1A: 3" × 18½" (1)
1B: 7½" × 1½" (1)
1C: 2½" × 1½" (1)
1D: 2½" × 6½" (1)
1E: 2½" × 2½" (1)

1F: 2½" × 1" (2)
1G: 1" × 1"
(16)—use stitch
and flip method
2A: 1½" × 17½" (1)

2B: 6½" × 6" (2)
3A: 1" × 18½" (1)
3B: 2½" × 2½" (4)

Caboose (18½" × 12½" unfinished)

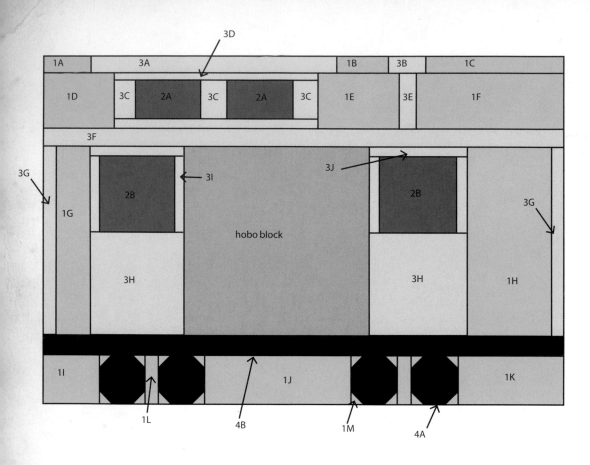

1A: 1" × 1½" (1)
1B: 1" × 2" (1)
1C: 1" × 4½" (1)
1D: 3" × 2½" (1)
1E: 3" × 3½" (1)
1F: 3" × 5" (1)

1G: 6½" × 2" (1)
1H: 6½" × 3½" (1)
1I: 2½" × 2¼" (1)
1J: 2½" × 4¼" (1)
1K: 2½" × 4" (1)
1L: 2½" × 1" (2)

IM: 1" × 1"
(16)—use stitch
and flip method
2A: 2½" × 3½" (2)
2B: 3" × 3¼" (2)
3A: 1" × 10" (1)

3B: 1" × 2½" (1)
3C: 2" × 1" (3)
3D: ¾" × 8" (2)
3E: 3" × 1½" (1)
3F: 1" × 18½" (1)
3G: 6½" × 1" (2)

3H: 3¾" × 3¾" (2)
3I: 3" × ¾" (4)
3J: ¾" × 3¾" (2)
4A: 2½" × 2½" (4)
4B: 1" × 18½" (1)

The Side Door Pullmans

Sometimes people get too fretful and a little bit forgetful,
Of the things we used to do in days gone by,
Once a friend in high good humor, said I used to be a boomer,
Have you ever caught a freight train on the fly?
For a while I thought about it, and I've caught 'em, don't you doubt it,
Then I answered truly, yes, I have caught some.
He said back when you were younger, have you ever known the hunger,
That you never know until you're on the bum.
I remember I have eaten hobo stew that can't be beaten,
By a little campfire in a misty rain,
There is nothing any better, where you're wet and gettin' wetter,
Than a Mulligan while waitin' for a train.
Have you seen and felt the starkness of a countryside in darkness,
Steppin' down the tracks on every other tie?
When the railroad bulls were diehards, keepin' you outside the freight yards
Where you caught a side-door Pullman on the fly.
Yes, I've waited by the trestle, listenin' for that highball whistle,
With the engine workin' up a head of steam.
When you hear that whistle blowin', soon you know that she'll be goin',
Down the track you see the headlight start to gleam.
There's a handy little grab bar on the front end of a boxcar,
Hold it tightly when you slam into the side,
On the rear end there's another, don't you ever grab it brother,
You'll be thrown between the cars for your last ride.
When you hear that old freight comin', down the tracks you're off and runnin',
Then you jump up like you're reachin' for the sky,
When you see that black smoke streamin' and you hear the whistle screamin',
Then you know you've caught a fast one on the fly.
This was in the great depression, those days make a deep impression,
When you used to catch a freight train rollin' by,
Now I'm old, I don't deny it and I wouldn't even try it.
But I used to like to catch one on the fly.

Photograph courtesy of the Library of Congress,
LC-DIG-GGBAIN-00405

Jack Cash,
California

HOBO JUNGLE

My inspiration for this quilt was to imagine a Jungle at dusk: I saw camp fires at random intervals (yellow stars), drinking water (blue diamonds) surrounded by grass (green accents) and hobos dressed in brown and red.

Materials List
for 48" × 48" Lap Quilt

16 Hobo Blocks of your choice pieced from scrap fabric
Blue Accent Fabric: ½ yard
Green Accent Fabric: 1 yard
Yellow Accent Fabric: ⅓ yard
Sashing and Inner Border: ⅝ yard
Outer Border: ⅔ yard
Binding: ⅜ yard
Backing: 1½ yards
Batting: 54" × 54"

Materials List
for 59" × 81" Twin Quilt

35 Hobo Blocks of your choice pieced from scrap fabric
Blue Accent Fabric: 1⅛ yards
Green Accent Fabric: 2 yards
Yellow Accent Fabric: ½ yard
Sashing and Inner Border: 1⅓ yards
Outer Border: 1⅛ yards
Binding: ⅔ yard
Backing: 5 yards
Batting: 65" × 87"

Materials List
for 81" × 103" Full Quilt

63 Hobo Blocks of your choice pieced from scrap fabric
Blue Accent Fabric: 1⅞ yards
Green Accent Fabric: 3⅝ yards
Yellow Accent Fabric: ½ yard
Sashing and Inner Border: 3 yards
Outer Border: 1⅛ yards
Binding: ¾ yard
Backing: 7¼ yards
Batting: 87" × 109"

DESIGNED AND PIECED BY DEBRA HENNINGER, QUILTED BY SHERRIE COPPENBARGER

Cutting List
for 48" × 48" Lap Quilt

Cut 3 strips 4½" × wof from Blue Accent Fabric, then from these strips cut the following:
> 24 4½" squares

Cut 3 strips 4½" × wof from Green Accent Fabric, then from these strips cut the following:
> 6 4½" squares
> 36 strips 4½" × 1½"

Cut 5 strips 2½" × wof from Green Accent Fabric, then from these strips cut the following:
> 74 2½" squares

Cut 1 strip 4½" × wof from Yellow Accent Fabric, then from this strip cut the following:
> 3 4½" squares
> 12 strips 4½" × 1½"

Cut 2 strips 2½" × wof from Yellow Accent Fabric, then from these strips cut the following:
> 24 2½" squares

Cut 17 strips 1" × wof for Sashing and Inner Border, then from these strips cut the following:
> 24 strips 1" × 6½"
> 18 strips 1" × 4½"
> 8 strips 1" × 39½"
> 2 strips 1" × 40½"

Cut 5 strips 4½" × wof for Outer Border, sew together into one strip, then from this strip cut the following:
> 2 strips 4½" × 40½"
> 2 strips 4½" × 48½"

Cutting List
for 59" × 81" Twin Quilt

Cut 8 strips 4½" × wof from Blue Accent Fabric, then from these strips cut the following:
> 58 4½" squares

Cut 7 strips 4½" × wof from Green Accent Fabric, then from these strips cut the following:
> 20 4½" squares
> 100 strips 4½" × 1½"

Cut 13 strips 2½" × wof from Green Accent Fabric, then from these strips cut the following:
> 200 2½" squares

Cut 2 strips 4½" × wof from Yellow Accent Fabric, then from this strip cut the following:
> 4 4½" squares
> 16 strips 4½" × 1½"

Cut 3 strips 2½" × wof from Yellow Accent Fabric, then from these strips cut the following:
> 32 2½" squares

Cut 39 strips 1" × wof for Sashing and Inner Border, sew together into one strip, then from this strip cut the following:
> 56 strips 1" × 6½"
> 48 strips 1" × 4½"
> 14 strips 1" × 50½"
> 2 strips 1" × 73½"

Cut 8 strips 4½" × wof for Outer Border, sew together into one strip, then from this strip cut the following:
> 2 strips 4½" × 59½"
> 2 strips 4½" × 73½"

Cutting List
for 81" × 103" Full Quilt

Cut 14 strips 4½" × wof from Blue Accent Fabric, then from these strips cut the following:
> 110 4½" squares

Cut 14 strips 4½" × wof from Green Accent Fabric, then from these strips cut the following:
> 42 4½" squares
> 196 strips 4½" × 1½"

Cut 25 strips 2½" × wof from Green Accent Fabric, then from these strips cut the following:
> 392 2½" squares

Cut 2 strips 4½" × wof from Yellow Accent Fabric, then from this strip cut the following:
> 6 4½" squares
> 24 strips 4½" × 1½"

Cut 3 strips 2½" × wof from Yellow Accent Fabric, then from these strips cut the following:
> 48 2½" squares

Cut 67 strips 1" × wof for Sashing and Inner Border, sew together into one strip, then from this strip cut the following:
> 108 strips 1" × 6½"
> 96 strips 1" × 4½"
> 18 strips 1" × 72½"
> 2 strips 1" × 95½"

Cut 8 strips 3½" × wof for Outer Border, sew together into one strip, then from this strip cut the following:
> 2 strips 3½" × 81½"
> 2 strips 3½" × 95½"

Assembly Instructions

- ▷ Using the stitch and flip method, sew a 2½" yellow square to each of 2 adjacent corners of a blue square (Fig. 1). Repeat 4 times for each yellow star. The Lap Quilt has 3 yellow stars; the Twin Quilt has 4 yellow stars; and the Full Quilt has 6 yellow stars.

- ▷ Sew a 4½" × 1½" yellow strip to the yellow end of each of the diamond blocks (Fig. 2).

- ▷ Stitch and flip the green 2½" squares to all remaining corners of all the blue squares. (Some will have 2 green corners and 2 yellow corners, most will have 4 green corners.)

- ▷ Sew a 4½" × 1½" green strip to the diamond blocks without a 4½" × 1½" yellow strip (Fig. 3). All blocks should now measure 4½" × 6½".

- ▷ Sew a 1" × 6½" sashing strip to each side of half the blocks with yellow corners. Sew the remaining 1" × 6½" sashing strips to each side of half the blocks with all green corners—half of the diamond blocks are without a sashing strip.

- ▷ Sew the 4½" × 1½" sashing strips to the 4½" sides of the diamond blocks that don't have sashing strips (Fig. 5).

- ▷ Lay out the even-numbered rows as shown in Fig. 6. Randomly place the 4½" yellow squares as star centers, use green for the remainder.

- ▷ Lay out the odd-numbered rows as shown in Fig. 7. Place the diamond blocks with yellow corners adjacent to the yellow star centers in the even-numbered rows. The Lap Quilt has 4 rows with 4 hobo blocks each, the Twin Quilt has 7 rows with 5 hobo blocks each and the Full Quilt has 9 rows with 7 hobo blocks each.

- ▷ Sew the shorter sashing strips between the rows, and to the top and bottom edges.

- ▷ Sew the rows together.

- ▷ Sew the longer sashing strips to each side.

- ▷ Sew the appropriate outer border strips to each side.

- ▷ Sew the appropriate outer border strips to the top and bottom edges.

- ▷ Quilt. Bind. Enjoy!

Fig. 1

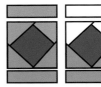

Fig. 2

Fig. 3

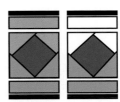

Fig. 4

Fig. 5

Fig. 6

Fig. 7

169

Photograph by Marion Post Wolcott, courtesy of the Library of Congress, lc-dig-ppmsc-00260

My folks had friends (played Bridge with them) and the man was in the Sherrif's Department and the only tale he had to tell was that our house number was written on a fence down in the Billings, Montana hobo jungle as a place where a fellow could always get a handout if he offered to work first. My mother gave askers a small sandwich and a cup of coffee first, then after they worked a bit, gave them a full meal on the steps leading up to our back porch. And a quarter. And then boiled their knife and fork and spoon and cup and plate or bowl after they left.

It was a damn difficult time. A humiliating time for many. We felt so sorry for all of them; sorrier for the cleaner, well spoken ones than for the guys who were awfully dirty and swore and used poor grammar, though. Small of us, huh?

— PAT O'CONNELL
Montana

YEGGS

In the hobo vernacular, a "yegg" was a thief, burglar or safe cracker. Most travelers were honest people, and they feared the yegg as much as everyone else.

Materials List
for 49½" × 66½" Throw Quilt

59 Hobo Blocks
White Block Fabric: 1⅝ yards
Red Block Fabric: 1⅞ yards
Light Gray Block Fabric: 1¼ yards
Dark Gray Block Fabric: ⅜ yard
Black Block Fabric: 1 yard
Side Setting Triangles: ⅝ yard
Corner Setting Triangles: ¼ yard
Inner Border: ⅓ yard
Outer Border: ⅝ yard
Binding: ⅝ yard
Backing: 3¼ yards
Batting: 56" × 72"

Cutting List
for 49½" × 66½" Throw Quilt

Cut 5 9¾" squares for Side Setting Triangles, then cut these squares in half diagonally twice for 20 quarter-square triangles

Cut 2 5⅛" squares for Corner Setting Triangles, then cut these squares in half diagonally for 4 half-square triangles

Cut 6 strips 1½" × WOF for Inner Border, sew together into one strip, then from this strip cut the following:
- 2 strips 1½" × 45"
- 2 strips 1½" × 60"

Cut 6 strips 3" × WOF for Outer Border, sew together into one strip, then from this strip cut the following:
- 2 strips 3" × 50"
- 2 strips 3" × 62"

Materials List
for 58" × 75" Lap Quilt

83 Hobo Blocks
White Block Fabric: 2⅛ yards
Red Block Fabric: 2½ yards
Light Gray Block Fabric: 1½ yards
Dark Gray Block Fabric: ¼ yard
Black Block Fabric: 1⅛ yards
Side Setting Triangles: ⅝ yard
Corner Setting Triangles: ¼ yard
Inner Border: ⅓ yard
Outer Border: ¾ yard
Binding: ⅝ yard
Backing: 3⅝ yards
Batting: 64" × 81"

Cutting List
for 58" × 75" Lap Quilt

Cut 6 9¾" squares for Side Setting Triangles, then cut these squares in half diagonally twice for 24 quarter-square triangles

Cut 2 5⅛" squares for Corner Setting Triangles, then cut these squares in half diagonally for 4 half-square triangles

Cut 7 strips 1½" × WOF for Inner Border, sew together into one strip, then from this strip cut the following:
- 2 strips 1½" × 53½"
- 2 strips 1½" × 68¼"

Cut 7 strips 3" × WOF for Outer Border, sew together into one strip, then from this strip cut the following:
- 2 strips 3" × 58½"
- 2 strips 3" × 70½"

Materials List
for 66½" × 83½" Twin Quilt

111 Hobo Blocks
White Block Fabric: 2¾ yards
Red Block Fabric: 3⅜ yards
Light Gray Block Fabric: 1⅞ yards
Dark Gray Block Fabric: ⅜ yard
Black Block Fabric: 1⅝ yards
Side Setting Triangles: ⅝ yard
Corner Setting Triangles: ¼ yard
Inner Border: ⅓ yard
Outer Border: ¾ yard
Binding: ⅔ yard
Backing: 5 yards
Batting: 73" × 90"

Cutting List
for 66½" × 83½" Twin Quilt

Cut 7 9¾" squares for Side Setting Triangles, then cut these squares in half diagonally twice for 28 quarter-square triangles

Cut 2 5⅛" squares for Corner Setting Triangles, then cut these squares in half diagonally for 4 half-square triangles

Cut 7 strips 1½" × WOF for Inner Border, sew together into one strip, then from this strip cut the following:
- 2 strips 1½" × 62"
- 2 strips 1½" × 77"

Cut 8 strips 3" × WOF for Outer Border, sew together into one strip, then from this strip cut the following:
- 2 strips 3" × 67"
- 2 strips 3" × 79"

DESIGNED BY DEBRA GREENWAY, PIECED BY JAN MISHLER, QUILTED BY JERI RENNIE

Materials List

179 Hobo Blocks
White Block Fabric: 4¼ yards
Red Block Fabric: 5½ yards
Light Gray Block Fabric: 2¾ yards
Dark Gray Block Fabric: ½ yard
Black Block Fabric: 2¼ yards
Side Setting Triangles: ⅞ yard
Corner Setting Triangles: ¼ yard
Inner Border: ½ yard
Outer Border: ⅞ yard
Binding: ⅞ yard
Backing: 7½ yards
Batting: 89" × 106"

Cutting List

for 83" × 100" Full Quilt

Cut 9 9¾" squares for Side Setting
Triangles, then cut these squares in half
diagonally twice for 36 quarter-square
triangles

Cut 2 5⅛" squares for Corner Setting
Triangles, then cut these squares in half
diagonally for 4 half-square triangles

Cut 9 strips 1½" × wof for Inner Border,
sew together into one strip, then from
this strip cut the following:
　　　2 strips 1½" × 79"
　　　2 strips 1½" × 94"

Cut 9 strips 3" × wof for Outer Border,
sew together into one strip, then from
this strip cut the following:
　　　2 strips 3" × 84"
　　　2 strips 3" × 96"

Materials List

for 92" × 109" Queen Quilt

219 Hobo Blocks
White Block Fabric: 5¼ yards
Red Block Fabric: 6¾ yards
Light Gray Block Fabric: 3⅜ yards
Dark Gray Block Fabric: ½ yard
Black Block Fabric: 2¾ yards
Side Setting Triangles: ⅞ yard
Corner Setting Triangles: ¼ yard
Inner Border: ½ yard
Outer Border: 1 yard
Binding: ⅞ yard
Backing: 8¼ yards
Batting: 98" × 115"

Cutting List

for 92" × 109" Queen Quilt

Cut 10 9¾" squares for Side Setting
Triangles, then cut these squares in half
diagonally twice for 40 quarter-square
triangles

Cut 2 5⅛" squares for Corner Setting
Triangles, then cut these squares in half
diagonally for 4 half-square triangles

Cut 10 strips 1½" × wof for Inner
Border, sew together into one strip, then
from this strip cut the following:
　　　2 strips 1½" × 87½"
　　　2 strips 1½" × 102½"

Cut 10 strips 3" × wof for Outer Border,
sew together into one strip, then from
this strip cut the following:
　　　2 strips 3" × 92½"
　　　2 strips 3" × 104½"

Assembly Instructions

▷ Assemble the hobo blocks for the quilt size of your choice. The example shown here uses the following blocks: Easy Mark (page 72), Jail (page 104), Danger (page 52) and Cowards—Will Give to Get Rid of You blocks (page 50). The Throw Quilt has 18 Easy Mark blocks, 12 Jail blocks, 12 Danger blocks and 17 Cowards—Will Give to Get Rid of You blocks; the Lap Quilt has 24 Easy Mark blocks, 17 Jail blocks, 18 Danger blocks and 24 Cowards—Will Give to Get Rid of You blocks; the Twin Quilt has 32 Easy Mark blocks, 24 Jail blocks, 24 Danger blocks and 31 Cowards—Will Give to Get Rid of You blocks; the Full Quilt has 50 Easy Mark blocks, 40 Jail blocks, 40 Danger blocks and 49 Cowards—Will Give to Get Rid of You blocks; the Queen Quilt has 60 Easy Mark blocks, 49 Jail blocks, 50 Danger blocks and 60 Cowards—Will Give to Get Rid of You blocks.

▷ Lay out the quilt top using the appropriate diagram below as your guide (Figs. 1 and 2). Start by laying out the corner blocks, then alternating Rows A and B, working toward the center row (see the photo on page 172 for the complete layout of the Twin quilt). The Twin Quilt has 5 Row A and 4 Row B; the Lap Quilt has 6 Row A and 5 Row B; the Twin Quilt has 7 Row A and 6 Row B; the Full Quilt has 9 Row A and 8 Row B; the Queen Quilt has 10 Row A and 9 Row B.

▷ Sew the blocks into rows.

▷ Sew a side setting triangle to the end of each row.

▷ Sew the rows together, making sure the side setting triangles match to make a straight edge.

▷ Sew a corner setting triangle to each corner.

▷ Sew a long inner border strip to each side of the quilt.

▷ Sew a short inner border strip to the top and bottom of the quilt.

▷ Sew a long outer border strip to each side of the quilt.

▷ Sew a short outer border strip to the top and bottom of the quilt.

▷ Quilt. Bind. Enjoy!

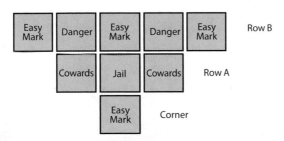

Fig. 1 (Throw, Twin and Full)

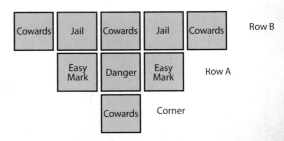

Fig. 2 (Lap and Queen)

Two fellow travelers invited me to share their humble breakfast. Al, a tall, flaxen-haired Canadian, had jumped the border at Winnipeg and was headed for Frisco to try for a job appearing in stock. Tony, an Italian who had been run out of Chicago as an unsavory character, was very proud of his collection of newspaper clippings about himself which he carried in his shoes.

The three of us strolled into Reno and looked the town over, but what can a fellow do with ten cents in the lining of his hat? Later we wandered down to the station. A railroad plainclothesman was kind enough to tell us we would receive thirty days on the road gang if we tried to board the overland Limited. I thanked him kindly and strolled down the track as the engineer gave the highball and the train gathered speed. I ran quickly to grab the engine ladder step. I was jerked straight out into the air like a flag waving in a strong wind. My buddies pulled me onto the engine.

The Limited began to climb slowly up the Sierra Nevadas, through green mountains of pine, with Lake Tahoe a deep, cold blue in the distance. As the train wound around a horseshoe curve, we could almost touch the people sitting on the observation platform. Tony said people were suckers to ride the cushions and have to pay, while we had a better view and no conductor to bother us for tickets.

We hopped off as we reached Truckee and hid in some bushes, waiting for the overland to highball. With the shriek of its whistle, we began running for our seats, but we were met by a reception committee: two railroad cops, who proceeded to stomp on our fingers as we grabbed for the rung of the engine ladder. The train stopped. We ran around to the other side, followed by the cops. We climbed up on the engine, but the cops were on to our trick and cut off our escape. Al began running over the top of the coaches as the train started again. We followed madly, with the cops running alongside on the tracks below. When we were almost the observation car, there to be cornered like rats, we heard the scream of a fast freight as it come up beside us, headed in the same direction. In a split second, Tony cried, "Let's go!" With a running leap, he landed on the moving freight car. Al followed, but I hesitated. It flashed through my mind what would happen if I didn't make the jump safely; Potter's field for me. Suddenly, I ran along the top of the coach, swerved with a high, forward leap in the air. What a wonderful feeling to hug that boxcar, and look back as we left the Limited and our dear enemies far in the distance. Once again we settled down on our Limited to continue our journey west.

RICHARD J. BUSSELL,
California

Photograph by Jack Delano, Courtesy of the Library of Congress, LC-USW3-020717-E

JACKROLLERS

A "jackroller" was a thief who often targeted hobos (or migrant workers) who had just received their pay.

Materials List
for 34" × 46" Wall Hanging Quilt

24 Hobo Blocks (Hit the Road Fast, page 94)
White Block Fabric: ½ yard
Light Gray Block Fabric: ½ yard
Dark Gray Block Fabric: ½ yard
Red Block Fabric: ⅝ yard
Inner Border: ¼ yard
Outer Border: ⅔ yard
Binding: ½ yard
Backing: 1½ yards
Batting: 40" × 52"

Cutting List
for 34" × 46" Wall Hanging Quilt

Cut 4 strips 1½" × WOF for Inner Border, then from these strips cut the following:
    2 strips 1½" × 26½"
    2 strips 1½" × 36½"

Cut 4 strips 4½" × WOF for Outer Border, then from these strips cut the following:
    2 strips 4½" × 34½"
    2 strips 4½" × 38½"

Materials List
for 46" × 58" Throw Quilt

48 Hobo Blocks (Hit the Road Fast, page 94)
White Block Fabric: ¾ yard
Light Gray Block Fabric: ⅝ yard
Dark Gray Block Fabric: ¾ yard
Red Block Fabric: 1⅛ yards
Inner Border: ⅓ yard
Outer Border: ⅞ yard
Binding: ⅝ yard
Backing: 3 yards
Batting: 52" × 64"

Cutting List
for 46" × 58" Throw Quilt

Cut 5 strips 1½" × WOF for Inner Border, sew together into one strip, then from this strip cut the following:
    2 strips 1½" × 38½"
    2 strips 1½" × 48½"

Cut 6 strips 4½" × WOF for Outer Border, sew together into one strip, then from this strip cut the following:
    2 strips 4½" × 46½"
    2 strips 4½" × 50½"

Materials List
for 58" × 70" Lap Quilt

80 Hobo Blocks (Hit the Road Fast, page 94)
White Block Fabric: 1⅛ yards
Light Gray Block Fabric: 1 yard
Dark Gray Block Fabric: ⅞ yard
Red Block Fabric: 1¾ yards
Inner Border: ⅜ yard
Outer Border: 1 yard
Binding: ⅝ yard
Backing: 3⅝ yards
Batting: 64" × 76"

Cutting List
for 58" × 70" Lap Quilt

Cut 6 strips 1½" × WOF for Inner Border, sew together into one strip, then from this strip cut the following:
    2 strips 1½" × 50½"
    2 strips 1½" × 60½"

Cut 7 strips 4½" × WOF for Outer Border, sew together into one strip, then from this strip cut the following:
    2 strips 4½" × 58½"
    2 strips 4½" × 62½"

Designed by Debra Greenway, Pieced by Wendy Russell, Quilted by Diana Snyder

Materials List
for 70" × 82" Twin Quilt

120 Hobo Blocks (Hit the Road Fast, page 94)
White Block Fabric: 1½ yards
Light Gray Block Fabric: 1⅜ yards
Dark Gray Block Fabric: 1¼ yards
Red Block Fabric: 2½ yards
Inner Border: ½ yard
Outer Border: 1⅛ yards
Binding: ⅔ yard
Backing: 5 yards
Batting: 76" × 88"

Cutting List
for 70" × 82" Twin Quilt

Cut 7 strips 1½" × WOF for Inner Border, sew together into one strip, then from this strip cut the following:
    2 strips 1½" × 62½"
    2 strips 1½" × 72½"

Cut 8 strips 4½" × WOF for Outer Border, sew together into one strip, then from this strip cut the following:
    2 strips 4½" × 70½"
    2 strips 4½" × 74½"

Assembly Instructions

▷ Arrange the blocks into sets of 4, 2 wide by 2 long, so that the long diagonals form a diamond (Fig. 1).

Fig. 1

Materials List
for 82" × 94" Full Quilt

168 Hobo Blocks (Hit the Road Fast, page 94)
White Block Fabric: 2 yards
Light Gray Block Fabric: 1¾ yards
Dark Gray Block Fabric: 1⅝ yards
Red Block Fabric: 3⅜ yards
Inner Border: ½ yard
Outer Border: 1¼ yards
Binding: ¾ yard
Backing: 7⅓ yards
Batting: 88" × 100"

Cutting List
for 82" × 94" Full Quilt

Cut 8 strips 1½" × WOF for Inner Border, sew together into one strip, then from this strip cut the following:
    2 strips 1½" × 74½"
    2 strips 1½" × 84½"

Cut 9 strips 4½" × WOF for Outer Border, sew together into one strip, then from this strip cut the following:
    2 strips 4½" × 82½"
    2 strips 4½" × 86½"

▷ Sew the blocks into rows. The Wall Hanging Quilt has 6 rows of 4 blocks; the Throw Quilt has 8 rows of 6 blocks; the Lap Quilt has 10 rows of 8 blocks; the Twin Quilt has 12 rows of 10 blocks; the Full Quilt has 14 rows of 12 blocks; and the Queen Quilt has 16 rows of 14 blocks.

▷ Sew the rows together to complete the inner quilt top.

Materials List
for 94" × 106" Queen Quilt

224 Hobo Blocks (Hit the Road Fast, page 94)
White Block Fabric: 2⅝ yards
Light Gray Block Fabric: 2¼ yards
Dark Gray Block Fabric: 2 yards
Red Block Fabric: 4⅜ yards
Inner Border: ½ yard
Outer Border: 1½ yards
Binding: ⅞ yard
Backing: 8⅓ yards
Batting: 100" × 110"

Cutting List
for 94" × 106" Queen Quilt

Cut 10 strips 1½" × WOF for Inner Border, sew together into one strip, then from this strip cut the following:
    2 strips 1½" × 86½"
    2 strips 1½" × 94½"

Cut 11 strips 4½" × WOF for Outer Border, sew together into one strip, then from this strip cut the following:
    2 strips 4½" × 94½"
    2 strips 4½" × 98½"

▷ Sew the longer inner border strips to the sides of the quilt.

▷ Sew the shorter inner border strips to the top and bottom of the quilt.

▷ Sew the longer outer border strips to the sides of the quilt.

▷ Sew the shorter outer border strips to the top and bottom of the quilt.

▷ Quilt. Bind. Enjoy!

I learned mostly the hard way—trial and failure, but lots of advice was given by older 'bos. Found out not to ride on front of a lumber car, as it would crush one on a sudden stop.

 William L. Pion,
Ohio

KNEE-SHAKER

Hobos were rarely invited inside to eat at a table. A "knee-shaker" refers to a handout on a plate at the back door of a house. The hobo would eat at the back steps while balancing the plate on his knees.

Materials List
for 44" × 50" Throw Quilt

30 Hobo Blocks (Housewife Feeds for Chores, page 100)
White Block Fabric: ½ yard
Black Block Fabric: ⅞ yard
Red Block Fabric: ⅝ yard
Inner Border: ¼ yard
Outer Border: 1 yard
Binding: ½ yard
Backing: 2⅞ yards
Batting: 50" × 56"

Cutting List
for 44" × 50" Throw Quilt

Cut 4 strips 1½" × WOF for Inner Border, then from these strips cut the following:
  2 strips 1½" × 32½"
  2 strips 1½" × 36½"

Cut 5 strips 6½" × WOF for Outer Border, sew together into one strip, then from this strip cut the following:
  2 strips 6½" × 38½"
  2 strips 6½" × 44½"

Materials List
for 56" × 68" Lap Quilt

63 Hobo Blocks (Housewife Feeds for Chores, page 100)
White Block Fabric: ⅞ yard
Black Block Fabric: 1⅝ yards
Red Block Fabric: 1⅛ yards
Inner Border: ⅜ yard
Outer Border: 1⅜ yards
Binding: ⅝ yard
Backing: 3½ yards
Batting: 62" × 74"

Cutting List
for 56" × 68" Lap Quilt

Cut 5 strips 1½" × WOF for Inner Border, sew together into one strip, then from this strip cut the following:
  2 strips 1½" × 44½"
  2 strips 1½" × 54½"

Cut 7 strips 6½" × WOF for Outer Border, sew together into one strip, then from this strip cut the following:
  4 strips 6½" × 56½"

Materials List
for 68" × 86" Twin Quilt

108 Hobo Blocks (Housewife Feeds for Chores, page 100)
White Block Fabric: 1⅜ yards
Black Block Fabric: 2⅝ yards
Red Block Fabric: 1¾ yards
Inner Border: ⅜ yard
Outer Border: 1⅝ yards
Binding: ⅔ yard
Backing: 5⅛ yards
Batting: 74" × 90"

Cutting List
for 68" × 86" Twin Quilt

Cut 7 strips 1½" × WOF for Inner Border, sew together into one strip, then from this strip cut the following:
  2 strips 1½" × 56½"
  2 strips 1½" × 72½"

Cut 8 strips 6½" × WOF for Outer Border, sew together into one strip, then from this strip cut the following:
  2 strips 6½" × 68½"
  2 strips 6½" × 74½"

DESIGNED BY DEBRA GREENWAY, PIECED BY WENDY RUSSELL, QUILTED BY SUZ TEALBY

Materials List
for 86" × 98" Full Quilt

168 Hobo Blocks (Housewife Feeds for Chores, page 100)
White Block Fabric: 2 yards
Black Block Fabric: 4 yards
Red Block Fabric: 2½ yards
Inner Border: ½ yard
Outer Border: 1⅞ yards
Binding: ¾ yard
Backing: 7¾ yards
Batting: 92" × 104"

Cutting List
for 86" × 98" Full Quilt

Cut 8 strips 1½" × WOF for Inner Border, sew together into one strip, then from this strip cut the following:
 2 strips 1½" × 74½"
 2 strips 1½" × 84½"

Cut 10 strips 6½" × WOF for Outer Border, sew together into one strip, then from this strip cut the following:
 4 strips 6½" × 86½"

Materials List
for 92" × 104" Queen Quilt

195 Hobo Blocks (Housewife Feeds for Chores, page 100)
White Block Fabric: 2¼ yards
Black Block Fabric: 4⅝ yards
Red Block Fabric: 2⅞ yards
Inner Border: ½ yard
Outer Border: 2⅛ yards
Binding: ⅞ yard
Backing: 8¼ yards
Batting: 98" × 110"

Cutting List
for 92" × 104" Queen Quilt

Cut 9 strips 1½" × WOF for Inner Border, sew together into one strip, then from this strip cut the following:
 2 strips 1½" × 80½"
 2 strips 1½" × 90½"

Cut 11 strips 6½" × WOF for Outer Border, sew together into one strip, then from this strip cut the following:
 4 strips 6½" × 92½"

Assembly Instructions

▷ Arrange the pieced blocks into rows, alternating the direction of every other block. The Throw Quilt has 6 rows of 5 blocks; the Lap Quilt has 9 rows of 7 blocks; the Twin Quilt has 12 rows of 9 blocks; the Full Quilt has 14 rows of 12 blocks; and the Queen Quilt has 15 rows of 13 blocks.

▷ Sew the blocks into rows.

▷ Sew the rows together to complete the inner quilt top.

▷ Sew the longer inner border strips to the sides of the quilt.

▷ Sew the shorter inner border strips to the top and bottom of the quilt.

▷ Sew the longer outer border strips to the sides of the quilt.

▷ Sew the shorter outer border strips to the top and bottom of the quilt.

▷ Quilt. Bind. Enjoy!

My father was a Station Agent for the Pennsylvania Railroad. I spent many hours at the station with my dad and saw lots of hobos. Mother would always feed them. Dad and I took lots of walks on his lunch hour and would see these individuals camping in the woods alongside the railroad tracks. I would immediately go back to Mother and she would pack food for them and Dad and I would take it to them.

Maybe their stay would be several days and then they'd be on their way. I would always cry when that happened because I claimed them as "friends." They were completely harmless but that was their way of life.

DOROTHY VORHAUER,
Virginia

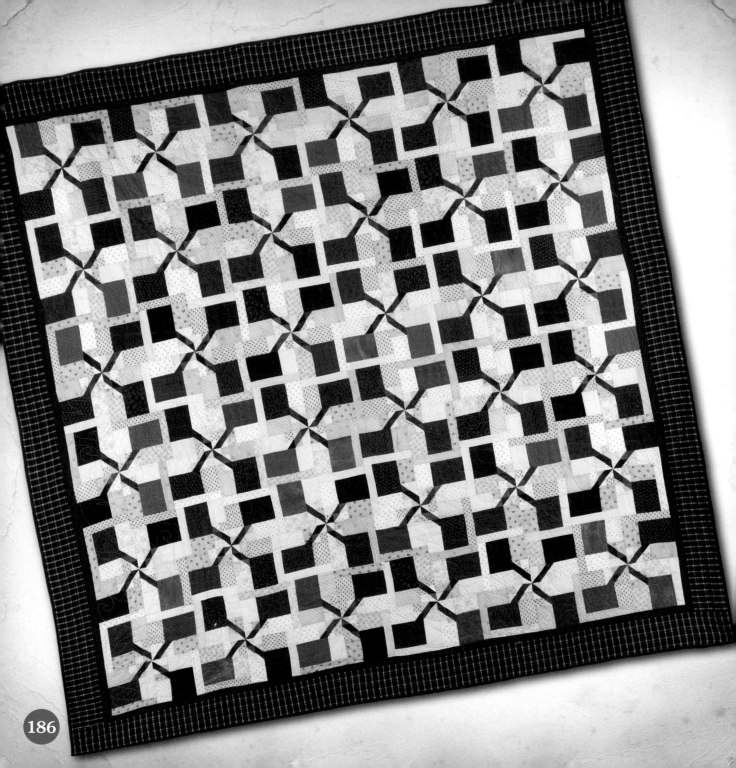

CANNED HEAT

"Canned heat" refers to the way hard-core drinking hobos would strain Sterno through a cloth to squeeze the alcohol from the paraffin. It was a very dangerous practice, and most travelers stayed as far away from them as possible.

Materials List
for 46" × 46" Crib Quilt

36 Hobo Blocks (Town Allows Alcohol, page 138)
Light Block Fabric: 1⅛ yards
Dark Block Fabric: ⅞ yard
Inner Border: ¼ yard
Outer Border: ¾ yard
Binding: ⅜ yard
Backing: 2⅞ yards
Batting: 54" × 54"

Cutting List
for 46" × 46" Crib Quilt

Cut 4 strips 1½" × WOF for Inner Border, then from these strips cut the following:
    2 strips 1½" × 36½"
    2 strips 1½" × 38½"

Cut 5 strips 4½" × WOF for Outer Border, sew together into one strip, then from this strip cut the following:
    2 strips 4½" × 38½"
    2 strips 4½" × 46½"

Materials List
for 58" × 58" Lap Quilt

64 Hobo Blocks (Town Allows Alcohol, page 138)
Light Block Fabric: 1⅞ yards
Dark Block Fabric: 1⅜ yards
Inner Border: ¼ yard
Outer Border: ⅞ yard
Binding: ½ yard
Backing: 3⅜ yards
Batting: 66" × 66"

Cutting List
for 58" × 58" Lap Quilt

Cut 5 strips 1½" × WOF for Inner Border, sew together into one strip, then from this strip cut the following:
    2 strips 1½" × 48½"
    2 strips 1½" × 50½"

Cut 6 strips 4½" × WOF for Outer Border, sew together into one strip, then from this strip cut the following:
    2 strips 4½" × 50½"
    2 strips 4½" × 58½"

Materials List
for 70" × 70" Twin Quilt

100 Hobo Blocks (Town Allows Alcohol, page 138)
Light Block Fabric: 2⅞ yards
Dark Block Fabric: 2 yards
Inner Border: ⅓ yard
Outer Border: 1 yard
Binding: ⅝ yard
Backing: 4⅓ yards
Batting: 76" × 76"

Cutting List
for 70" × 70" Twin Quilt

Cut 7 strips 1½" × WOF for Inner Border, sew together into one strip, then from this strip cut the following:
    2 strips 1½" × 60½"
    2 strips 1½" × 62½"

Cut 8 strips 4½" × WOF for Outer Border, sew together into one strip, then from this strip cut the following:
    2 strips 4½" × 62½"
    2 strips 4½" × 70½"

Designed by Debra Henninger, Pieced by Theresa Cobb, Quilted by Diana Snyder

Materials List
for 82" × 82" Full Quilt

144 Hobo Blocks (Town Allows Alcohol, page 138)
Light Block Fabric: 4⅛ yards
Dark Block Fabric: 2⅞ yards
Inner Border: ⅜ yard
Outer Border: 1¼ yards
Binding: ¾ yard
Backing: 7⅓ yards
Batting: 88" × 88"

Cutting List
for 82" × 82" Full Quilt

Cut 8 strips 1½" × WOF for Inner Border, sew together into one strip, then from this strip cut the following:
 2 strips 1½" × 72½"
 2 strips 1½" × 74½"

Cut 9 strips 4½" × WOF for Outer Border, sew together into one strip, then from this strip cut the following:
 2 strips 4½" × 74½"
 2 strips 4½" × 82½"

Materials List
for 94" × 94" Queen Quilt

196 Hobo Blocks (Town Allows Alcohol, page 138)
Light Block Fabric: 5⅛ yards
Dark Block Fabric: 3½ yards
Inner Border: ½ yard
Outer Border: 1⅜ yards
Binding: ⅞ yard
Backing: 8⅓ yards
Batting: 100" × 100"

Cutting List
for 94" × 94" Queen Quilt

Cut 9 strips 1½" × WOF for Inner Border, sew together into one strip, then from this strip cut the following:
 2 strips 1½" × 84½"
 2 strips 1½" × 86½"

Cut 10 strips 4½" × WOF for Outer Border, sew together into one strip, then from this strip cut the following:
 2 strips 4½" × 86½"
 2 strips 4½" × 94½"

Assembly Instructions

▷ Arrange the pieced blocks into sets of 4, 2 wide by 2 long, so an X forms at the intersection of the blocks (Fig. 1).

▷ Sew the blocks into rows. The Crib Quilt has 3 rows of 3 blocks; the Lap Quilt has 4 rows of 4 blocks; the Twin Quilt has 5 rows of 5 blocks; the Full Quilt has 6 rows of 6 blocks; and the Queen Quilt has 7 rows of 7 blocks.

▷ Sew the rows together to complete the inner quilt top.

▷ Sew the shorter inner border strips to the sides of the quilt.

▷ Sew the longer inner border strips to the top and bottom of the quilt.

▷ Sew the shorter outer border strips to the sides of the quilt.

▷ Sew the longer outer border strips to the top and bottom of the quilt.

▷ Quilt. Bind. Enjoy!

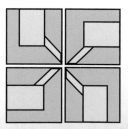
Fig. 1

On the way home we hitchhiked to Winona, Wisconsin. When we got there it was getting dark so we headed for the station to catch a train. There we met a young fellow that filled us in on tricks of travel. "Stay away from the hobo camps," he warned. "Those guys drink canned heat. Only last week one of them went crazy and started beating sleeping men on the head with a two by four."

CHARLES N. BISHOP,
California

Photograph courtesy of the Library of Congress, lc-dig-ggbain-00407

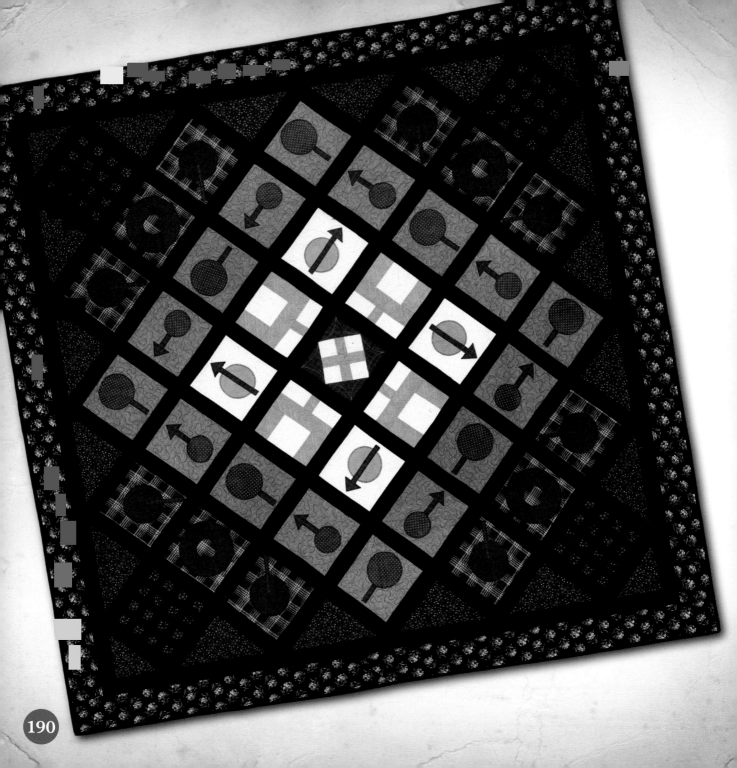

COURTESY CALL

Many hobos would ask to spend the night at the jail where they would find a dry, warm place to sleep. If they were lucky, the jailer would give them a meal while there. Many jailers would allow such "courtesy calls" if they had an empty cell.

Materials List
for 62" × 62" Quilt

41 Hobo Blocks
Sashing: 1¼ yards
Side Setting Triangles: ⅝ yard
Corner Setting Triangles: ¼ yard
Inner Border: ⅜ yard
Outer Border: ⅝ yard
Binding: ⅝ yard
Backing: 3⅞ yards
Batting: 68" × 68"

Cutting List
for 62" × 62" Quilt

Cut 22 strips 2" × WOF for Sashing, sew together into one strip, then from this strip cut the following:
    50 strips 2" × 6½"
    2 strips 2" × 9½"
    2 strips 2" × 24½"
    2 strips 2" × 39½"
    2 strips 2" × 54½"
    2 strips 2" × 69½"

Cut 4 9¾" squares for Side Setting Triangles, then cut these squares in half diagonally twice

Cut 2 5⅛" squares for Corner Setting Triangles, then cut these squares in half diagonally for 4 half-square triangles

Cut 6 strips 2" × WOF for Inner Border, sew together into one strip, then from this strip cut the following:
    2 strips 2" × 53½"
    2 strips 2" × 56½"

Cut 6 strips 3½" × WOF for Outer Border, sew together into one strip, then from this strip cut the following:
    2 strips 3½" × 56½"
    2 strips 3½" × 62½"

Designed by Debra Greenway, Pieced and Appliquéd by Claudette Cremer, Quilted by Sherrie Coppenbarger

Assembly Instructions

▷ Arrange the blocks as they will appear in the quilt. For this quilt I used the following blocks: OK (page 116); Here Is the Place (page 92); Don't Go This Way (page 66); Go this Way (page 84); Bad-Tempered Man (page 26); At the Crossroad, Go This Way (page 18); Jail (page 104); and Straight Ahead (page 132). Refer to the photo on page 190 if you'd like to arrange your quilt like the project shown.

▷ Sew a 6½" sashing strip to the left edge of each block, and to the right edge of the last block in each row. (Sashing strips are shown in white in the diagram.)

▷ Sew the blocks with sashing strips into rows.

▷ Sew a 9½" sashing strip to the top of Row 1 and the bottom of Row 9 (as shown in yellow).

▷ Sew a 24½" sashing strip to the top of Row 2 and the bottom of Row 8 (shown in orange).

▷ Sew a 39½" sashing strip to the top of Row 3 and the bottom of Row 7 (shown in red).

▷ Sew a 54½" sashing strip to the top of Row 4 and the bottom of Row 6 (shown in purple).

▷ Sew a 69½" strip to the top and bottom of Row 5 (shown in blue).

▷ Sew a setting triangle to each end of each row (as shown in green).

▷ Sew a corner setting triangle at each corner (as shown in pink).

▷ Sew the rows together to complete the inner quilt top.

▷ Square up the quilt top, trimming off the extra lengths at the end of each sashing strip. Be sure to leave a ¼" seam allowance.

▷ Sew the shorter inner border strips to each side of the quilt top.

▷ Sew the longer inner border strips to the top and bottom edges.

▷ Sew the shorter outer border strips to each side of the quilt top.

▷ Sew the longer outer border strips to the top and bottom edges.

▷ Quilt. Bind. Enjoy!

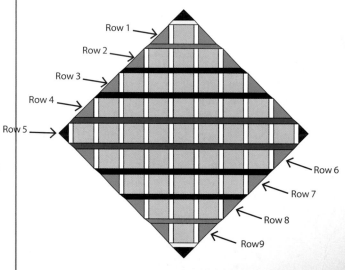

PHOTOGRAPH BY DOROTHEA LANGE, COURTESY OF THE LIBRARY OF CONGRESS, LC-DIG-FSA-8B32870

When going through a town the local police might pick you up on a vagrancy charge, let you sleep on the concrete floor in the jail house (at least it was warm) and let you out at the edge of town the next morning.

 Malcom D. Stewart,
Indiana

HIGH IRON

"High iron" is the track in a railroad yard that serves as the main line or through line. Knowing how a rail yard operated was essential information to the successful hobo.

Materials List
for 45" × 61" Throw Quilt

30 Hobo Blocks pieced from scrap fabric
(Catch out Here, page 42)
Plain Alternate Rows: ⅜ yard
Inner Border: ⅓ yard
Outer Border: 1½ yards
Binding: ½ yard
Backing: 3 yards
Batting: 51" × 67"

Cutting List
for 45" × 61" Throw Quilt

Cut 5 strips 2½" × WOF for Plain
Alternate Rows, then from these strips
cut the following:
     5 strips 2½" × 30½"

Cut 5 strips 2" × WOF for Inner Border,
sew together into one strip, then from
this strip cut the following:
     2 strips 2" × 33½"
     2 strips 2" × 46½"

Cut 8 strips 6½" × WOF for Outer
Border, sew together into one strip,
then from this strip cut the following:
     2 strips 6½" × 50"
     2 strips 6½" × 65"

Materials List
for 57" × 77" Lap Quilt

56 Hobo Blocks pieced from scrap fabric
(Catch out Here, page 42)
Plain Alternate Rows: ¾ yard
Inner Border: ⅜ yard
Outer Border: 1½ yards
Binding: ⅝ yard
Backing: 3½ yards
Batting: 63" × 83"

Cutting List
for 57" × 77" Lap Quilt

Cut 8 strips 2½" × WOF for Plain
Alternate Rows, sew together into
one strip, then from this strip cut
the following:
     7 strips 2½" × 42½"

Cut 6 strips 2" × WOF for Inner Border,
sew together into one strip, then from
this strip cut the following:
     2 strips 2" × 45½"
     2 strips 2" × 62½"

Cut 7 strips 6½" × WOF for Outer
Border, sew together into one strip,
then from this strip cut the following:
     2 strips 6½" × 60"
     2 strips 6½" × 80"

Materials List
for 69" × 85" Twin Quilt

81 Hobo Blocks pieced from scrap fabric
(Catch out Here, page 42)
Plain Alternate Rows: 1 yard
Inner Border: ½ yard
Outer Border: 1¾ yards
Binding: ⅔ yard
Backing: 5¼ yards
Batting: 75" × 91"

Cutting List
for 69" × 85" Twin Quilt

Cut 11 strips 2½" × WOF for Plain
Alternate Rows, sew together into
one strip, then from this strip cut
the following:
     8 strips 2½" × 54½"

Cut 7 strips 2" × WOF for Inner Border,
sew together into one strip, then from
this strip cut the following:
     2 strips 2" × 57½"
     2 strips 2" × 70½"

Cut 9 strips 6½" × WOF for Outer
Border, sew together into one strip,
then from this strip cut the following:
     2 strips 6½" × 72"
     2 strips 6½" × 88"

DESIGNED BY DEBRA HENNINGER, PIECED BY JAN MISHLER, QUILTED BY JAN MISHLER AND SHERRIE COPPENBARGER

Materials List
for 81" × 101" Full Quilt

121 Hobo Blocks pieced from scrap fabric (Catch out Here, page 42)
Plain Alternate Rows: 1⅓ yards
Inner Border: ⅝ yard
Outer Border: 2 yards
Binding: ¾ yard
Backing: 7¼ yards
Batting: 87" × 107"

Cutting List
for 81" × 101" Full Quilt

Cut 16 strips 2½" × WOF for Plain Alternate Rows, sew together into one strip, then from this strip cut the following:

> 10 strips 2½" × 66½"

Cut 8 strips 2" × WOF for Inner Border, sew together into one strip, then from this strip cut the following:

> 2 strips 2" × 69½"
> 2 strips 2" × 86½"

Cut 10 strips 6½" × WOF for Outer Border, sew together into one strip, then from this strip cut the following:

> 2 strips 6½" × 85"
> 2 strips 6½" × 105"

Materials List
for 87" × 101" Queen Quilt

132 Hobo Blocks pieced from scrap fabric (Catch out Here, page 42)
Plain Alternate Rows: 1½ yards
Inner Border: ⅝ yard
Outer Border: 2 yards
Binding: ¾ yard
Backing: 7¾ yards
Batting: 93" × 107"

Cutting List
for 87" × 101" Queen Quilt

Cut 19 strips 2½" × WOF for Plain Alternate Rows, sew together into one strip, then from this strip cut the following:

> 10 strips 2½" × 72½"

Cut 9 strips 2" × WOF for Inner Border, sew together into one strip, then from this strip cut the following:

> 2 strips 2" × 75½"
> 2 strips 2" × 86½"

Cut 10 strips 6½" × WOF for Outer Border, sew together into one strip, then from this strip cut the following:

> 2 strips 6½" × 90"
> 2 strips 6½" × 105"

Assembly Instructions

▷ Arrange the blocks into rows, alternating light and dark blocks. The Throw Quilt has 6 rows of 5 blocks; the Lap Quilt has 8 rows of 7 blocks; the Twin Quilt has 9 rows of 9 blocks; the Full Quilt has 11 rows of 11 blocks; and the Queen Quilt has 11 rows of 12 blocks.

▷ Sew the blocks into rows.

▷ Sew a plain row to the bottom of each train row except for the bottom row.

▷ Sew the rows together to complete the inner quilt top.

▷ Sew the long inner border strips to the sides of the quilt.

▷ Sew the short inner border strips to the top and bottom of the quilt.

▷ Using your favorite mitering technique, add the outer borders.

▷ Quilt. Bind. Enjoy!

PHOTOGRAPH BY DOROTHEA LANGE, COURTESY OF THE LIBRARY OF CONGRESS, LC-DIG-FSA-8B33233

In 1938 when I was four years old I was taken off the farm to Hillyard, Washington to my great aunt and uncle's house. On the way I saw ten to fifteen men dressed quite poorly, carrying their belongings in any way they could. Most had packs tied up with rope in such a way they could use the rope as handles. Hillyard was where the Great Northern Railroad roundhouse was located. It's where they turned the train around on a huge lazy susan type apparatus. As a matter of fact, my Uncle Jack worked there for a time and brought home a roundhouse door that we used as a porch off the kitchen. It was very large and I am sorry I never asked him how he got it home!

 JUANITA PENMAN,
Tennessee

In Montana and in North Dakota I saw many whole families getting on the train with all they could carry—men, women and children. The Yard Bulls in each Division town were very kind and told people where to go and what time the train would be leaving. They wanted people to keep going. I will never forget those poor, poor families.

HAROLD SPARKS,
Virginia

197

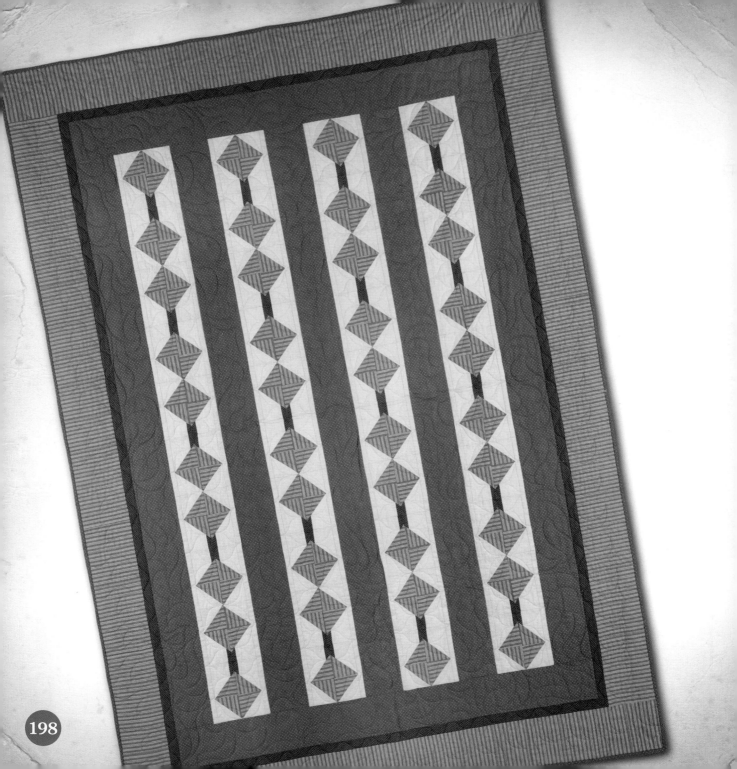

CINDER BULL

A railroad detective was commonly called a "dick" or "bull" or "cinder bull." These men were hired to keep trespassers off the trains, but especially out of the train yards.

Materials List
for 44" × 62" Throw Quilt

12 Hobo Blocks (Be Prepared to Defend Yourself, page 34)
Sashing Strips: 1 yard
Inner Border: ¼ yard
Outer Border: 1¼ yards
Binding: ½ yard
Backing: 2¾ yards
Batting: 52" × 70"

Cutting List
for 44" × 62" Throw Quilt

Cut 5 strips 6½" × WOF for Sashing Strips, then from these strips cut the following:
    3 strips 6½" × 36½"
    2 strips 6½" × 30½"

Cut 5 strips 1½" × WOF for Inner Border, then from these strips cut the following:
    2 strips 1½" × 48½"
    2 strips 1½" × 32½"

Cut 6 strips 6½" × WOF for Outer Border, sew together into one strip, then from this strip cut the following:
    2 strips 6½" × 50½"
    2 strips 6½" × 44½"

Materials List
for 68" × 86" Lap Quilt

40 Hobo Blocks (Be Prepared to Defend Yourself, page 34)
Sashing Strips: 2½ yards
Inner Border: ⅓ yard
Outer Border: ½ yard
Binding: ⅔ yard
Backing: 6¼ yards
Batting: 76" × 94"

Cutting List
for 68" × 86" Lap Quilt

Cut 12 strips 6½" × WOF for Sashing Strips, sew together into one strip, then from this strip cut the following:
    5 strips 6½" × 60½"
    2 strips 6½" × 54½"

Cut 6 strips 1½" × WOF for Inner Border, sew together into one strip, then from this strip cut the following:
    2 strips 1½" × 74½"
    2 strips 1½" × 56½"

Cut 6 strips 6½" × WOF for Outer Border, sew together into one strip, then from this strip cut the following:
    2 strips 6½" × 74½"
    2 strips 6½" × 68½"

Materials List
for 68" × 98" Twin Quilt

48 Hobo Blocks (Be Prepared to Defend Yourself, page 34)
Sashing Strips: 2 yards
Inner Border: ½ yard
Outer Border: 1¾ yards
Binding: ⅔ yard
Backing: 6¼ yards
Batting: 76" × 106"

Cutting List
for 68" × 98" Twin Quilt

Cut 11 strips 6½" × WOF for Sashing Strips, sew together into one strip, then from this strip cut the following:
    5 strips 6½" × 84½"
    2 strips 6½" × 54½"

Cut 8 strips 1½" × WOF for Inner Border, sew together into one strip, then from this strip cut the following:
    2 strips 1½" × 84½"
    2 strips 1½" × 56½"

Cut 9 strips 6½" × WOF for Outer Border, sew together into one strip, then from this strip cut the following:
    2 strips 6½" × 86½"
    2 strips 6½" × 68½"

Designed by Debra Henninger, Pieced by Connie Markley and Wendy Russell, Quilted by Sherrie Coppenbarger

Materials List

for 80" × 98" Full Quilt

84 Hobo Blocks (Be Prepared to Defend Yourself, page 34)
Sashing Strips: 3 yards
Inner Border: ½ yard
Outer Border: 1½ yards
Binding: ¾ yard
Backing: 7⅓ yards
Batting: 86" × 104"

Cutting List

for 80" × 98" Full Quilt

Cut 11 strips 6½" × wof for Sashing Strips, sew together into one strip, then from this strip cut the following:

      6 strips 6½" × 72½"
      2 strips 6½" × 66½"

Cut 8 strips 1½" × wof for Inner Border, sew together into one strip, then from this strip cut the following:

      2 strips 1½" × 68½"
      2 strips 1½" × 84½"

Cut 10 strips 6½" × wof for Outer Border, sew together into one strip, then from this strip cut the following:

      2 strips 6½" × 80½"
      2 strips 6½" × 86½"

Assembly Instructions

▷ Arrange the completed blocks into columns, flipping every other block vertically. The Throw Quilt has 2 columns of 6 blocks; the Lap Quilt has 4 columns of 10 blocks; the Twin Quilt has 4 columns of 12 blocks; and the Full Quilt has 5 columns of 12 blocks.

▷ Sew the blocks into columns.

▷ Arrange the quilt top with a sashing strip between each column and on the right and left sides of the quilt.

▷ Sew all of the columns and sashing strips together to complete the inner quilt top.

▷ Sew the shorter sashing strips to the top and bottom of the quilt.

▷ Sew the longer inner border strips to the sides of the quilt.

▷ Sew the shorter inner border strips to the top and bottom of the quilt.

▷ Sew the longer outer border strips to the sides of the quilt.

▷ Sew the shorter outer border strips to the top and bottom of the quilt.

▷ Quilt. Bind. Enjoy!

Once in Cincinnati, another guy and I were sitting by the track, near the Ohio River, waiting for a south-bound freight. A railroad dick came by and asked us if we were going south. We told him yes. He told us not to catch the first one, it was a manifest, to catch the second one. He walked on down towards the river. When the first freight pulled out, we caught it and the dick saw us. About 200 yards down the track we caught up with the dick. The dick pulled his pistol and fired several shot at us. Luck was with us, neither was hit.

JAMES L. BLACKMAN,
Missouri

HOOVERVILLE

"Hoovervilles" were shanty towns built by squatters using cardboard, tin and any other available materials.
The term was also used to refer to temporary housing (tents, empty boxcars or shacks) built for transients.

Materials List

for 32" × 50" Wall Hanging Quilt

28 Hobo Blocks
Inner Border: ¼ yard
Outer Border: ⅜ yards
Binding: ⅜ yard
Backing: 2¼ yards
Batting: 38" × 56"

Cutting List

for 32" × 50" Wall Hanging Quilt

Cut 4 strips 1½" × WOF for Inner Border, sew together into one strip, then from this strip cut the following:
    2 strips 1½" × 26½"
    2 strips 1½" × 42½"

Cut 5 strips 3½" × WOF for Outer Border, sew together into one strip, then from this strip cut the following:
    2 strips 3½" × 32½"
    2 strips 3½" × 44½"

Assembly Instructions

▷ Arrange the blocks as they will appear in the quilt. For this quilt, the first row is made from the Bad Drinking Water block (page 22); the second row is made from the Poor Man block (page 118); the third row has the Don't Go this Way (page 66), Hold Your Tongue (page 98), Doctor, No Charge (page 62) and You'll Get Cursed out Here (page 150) blocks; the fourth row is made from the Good Water block (page 90); the fifth row has the Dishonest Person Lives Here (page 60), Tell Pitiful Story (page 136), Man with a Gun (page 110) and Good Chance to Get Money (page 86) blocks; the sixth row is made from the Officer Lives Here block (page 114); the seventh row is made from the Keep Quiet block (page 106).

▷ Sew the blocks into rows, then sew the rows together.

▷ Sew the longer inner border strips to each side of the quilt.

▷ Sew the shorter inner border strips to the top and bottom of the quilt.

▷ Sew the longer outer border strips to each side of the quilt.

▷ Sew the shorter outer border strips to the top and bottom of the quilt.

▷ Quilt. Bind. Enjoy!

{ HELPFUL HINT }

This quilt is a great way to use up scraps. For my quilt, I varied the number of fabrics used in some of the blocks, but stuck with earth-toned fabrics to pull the blocks together.

It was at Lowell, Washington, that the Great Northern Railway coming west out of the Scenic Tunnel under Stevens Pass through the Cascades came to where it turned south to keep from running into Puget Sound, and continued on for another thirty miles south to Seattle. The big yards for what was a kind of western terminus were not in Seattle, but within walking distance of our house. On the other side of the tracks was an old abandoned shingle mill, which could be reached by an over-the-tracks foot bridge. We kids spent many an hour on that bridge watching freight trains and an occasional Empire Builder go magically under us. Sometimes it seemed like the train cars were standing still and we were flying over them.

In and on those freight cars were hundreds and hundreds of men from all over America, "riding the rails" in search of something better, or in some cases, simply survival.

My father was minister of the Lowell Community Church and active in community affairs. He worked with a group of community people to set up what came to be known as a "Hooverville" down by the tracks. There, anyone coming in from the freight trains could get a shower and de-lousing, their clothing laundered, three

square meals, and a night's sleep on a clean bed. Each person could stay twenty-four hours and then they had to move on. In charge of the operation was Slim. I never knew any other name. He came off a freight train himself and walked with a limp because one knee was stiff and permanently bent. He saw to it that the system worked and he was respected. The men were from all walks of life and all economic and educational backgrounds. One man said he'd be glad to trade his Ph.D. for a J O B!

Our little town had a paper mill that kept operating all the way through the depression, primarily because of foreign markets. We used to say that nobody was rich in our town, but because of the paper mill everybody had a job. And in the 1930s, that was one definition of being rich. So the townspeople gathered enough money to keep the Hooverville going for those who rode the rails. I'm kind of proud of that memory.

— CARL BAIRD,
Michigan

PHOTOGRAPH BY F. J. CONWAY, COURTESY OF THE LIBRARY OF CONGRESS, LC-USZ62-52782

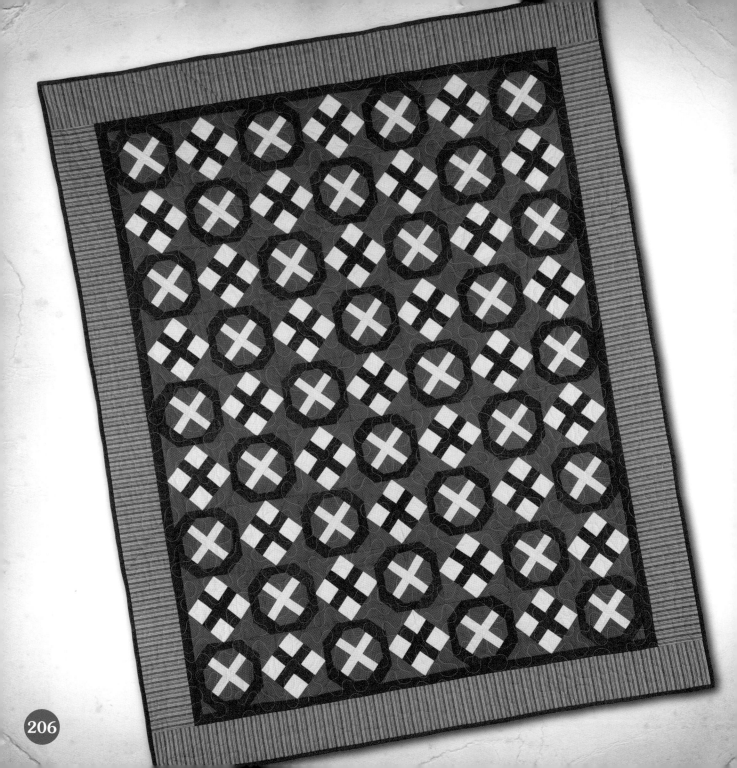

ON THE BUM

Tramp, hobo or bum, all were "on the bum"—living as vagrants and depending on hand-outs.

Materials List
for 46" × 52" Throw Quilt

42 Hobo Blocks
White Block Fabric: ⅝ yard
Red Block Fabric: 1⅜ yards
Green Block Fabric: 1¼ yards
Inner Border: ¼ yard
Outer Border: ¾ yard
Binding: ½ yard
Backing: 3 yards
Batting: 52" × 58"

Cutting List
for 46" × 52" Throw Quilt

Cut 4 strips 1½" × WOF for Inner Border, then from these strips cut the following:
  2 strips 1½" × 38½"
  2 strips 1½" × 42½"

Cut 5 strips 4½" × WOF for Outer Border, sew together into one strip, then from this strip cut the following:
  2 strips 4½" × 46½"
  2 strips 4½" × 44½"

Materials List
for 58" × 70" Lap Quilt

80 Hobo Blocks
White Block Fabric: 1⅛ yards
Red Block Fabric: 2⅜ yards
Green Block Fabric: 2⅛ yards
Inner Border: ⅓ yard
Outer Border: 1 yard
Binding: ⅝ yard
Backing: 3⅝ yards
Batting: 64" × 76"

Cutting List
for 58" × 70" Lap Quilt

Cut 6 strips 1½" × WOF for Inner Border, sew together into one strip, then from this strip cut the following:
  2 strips 1½" × 50½"
  2 strips 1½" × 60½"

Cut 7 strips 4½" × WOF for Outer Border, sew together into one strip, then from this strip cut the following:
  2 strips 4½" × 58½"
  2 strips 4½" × 62½"

Materials List
for 70" × 82" Twin Quilt

120 Hobo Blocks
White Block Fabric: 1½ yards
Red Block Fabric: 3¼ yards
Green Block Fabric: 3 yards
Inner Border: ⅜ yard
Outer Border: 1¼ yards
Binding: ⅔ yard
Backing: 5 yards
Batting: 76" × 88"

Cutting List
for 70" × 82" Twin Quilt

Cut 7 strips 1½" × WOF for Inner Border, sew together into one strip, then from this strip cut the following:
  2 strips 1½" × 62½"
  2 strips 1½" × 72½"

Cut 8 strips 4½" × WOF for Outer Border, sew together into one strip, then from this strip cut the following:
  2 strips 4½" × 70½"
  2 strips 4½" × 74½"

Designed by Debra Henninger, Pieced by Linda Ward, Alice Braman, and Georjean Lipovsky, Quilted by Barb Sidell

Materials List
for 82" × 94" Full Quilt

168 Hobo Blocks
White Block Fabric: 2 yards
Red Block Fabric: 4½ yards
Green Block Fabric: 4¼ yards
Inner Border: ½ yard
Outer Border: 1⅓ yards
Binding: ¾ yard
Backing: 7⅓ yards
Batting: 88" × 100"

Cutting List
for 82" × 94" Full Quilt

Cut 8 strips 1½" × WOF for Inner Border,
sew together into one strip, then from
this strip cut the following:
    2 strips 1½" × 74½"
    2 strips 1½" × 84½"

Cut 9 strips 4½" × WOF for Outer
Border, sew together into one strip,
then from this strip cut the following:
    2 strips 4½" × 82½"
    2 strips 4½" × 86½"

Materials List
for 94" × 106" Queen Quilt

224 Hobo Blocks
White Block Fabric: 2½ yards
Red Block Fabric: 5⅞ yards
Green Block Fabric: 5½ yards
Inner Border: ½ yard
Outer Border: 1½ yards
Binding: ⅞ yard
Backing: 8½ yards
Batting: 100" × 112"

Cutting List
for 94" × 106" Queen Quilt

Cut 10 strips 1½" × WOF for Inner
Border, sew together into one strip, then
from this strip cut the following:
    2 strips 1½" × 86½"
    2 strips 1½" × 96½"

Cut 11 strips 4½" × WOF for Outer
Border, sew together into one strip,
then from this strip cut the following:
    2 strips 4½" × 94½"
    2 strips 4½" × 98½"

Assembly Instructions

▷ Lay out the blocks into rows, alternating Good for a Handout blocks (page 88) and OK blocks (page 116). The Throw Quilt has 7 rows of 6 blocks; the Lap Quilt has 10 rows of 8 blocks; the Twin Quilt has 12 rows of 10 blocks; the Full Quilt has 14 rows of 12 blocks; and the Queen Quilt has 16 rows of 14 blocks.

▷ Sew the blocks into rows.

▷ Sew the rows together to complete the inner quilt top.

▷ Sew the longer inner border strips to each side of the quilt.

▷ Sew the shorter inner border strips to the top and bottom.

▷ Sew the longer outer border strips to each side of the quilt.

▷ Sew the shorter outer border strips to the top and bottom.

▷ Quilt. Bind. Enjoy!

One young 'bo showed me how to "ride the rods" on sealed trains. I did it once—never again. Cinders, gravel, etc., in all places, plus you must stay awake—if you fall it's certain death. (These are the iron rods that cross beneath the cars.)

WILLIAM L. PION,
Ohio

PHOTOGRAPH BY DOROTHEA LANGE, COURTESY OF THE LIBRARY OF CONGRESS, LC-DIG-FSA-8B31775

KNIGHTS OF THE ROAD

Being referred to as a "knight of the road" was a very respectful term that related to the honor and trustworthiness of most hobos.

Materials List
for 36" × 48" Wall Hanging Quilt

48 Hobo Blocks
Light Block Color: 1 yard
Dark Block Color: 1¼ yards
Binding: ⅜ yard
Backing: 2⅓ yards
Batting: 42" × 54"

Materials List
for 72" × 96" Twin Quilt

192 Hobo Blocks
Light Block Color: 3⅝ yards
Dark Block Color: 4¾ yards
Binding: ¾ yard
Backing: 5⅔ yards
Batting: 78" × 102"

Materials List
for 54" × 72" Lap Quilt

108 Hobo Blocks
Light Block Color: 2⅛ yards
Dark Block Color: 2⅝ yards
Binding: ⅝ yard
Backing: 3⅓ yards
Batting: 60" × 78"

Materials List
for 84" × 96" Full Quilt

224 Hobo Blocks
Light Block Color: 4⅛ yards
Dark Block Color: 5½ yards
Binding: ¾ yard
Backing: 7½ yards
Batting: 90" × 102"

Designed by Debra Greenway, Pieced and Quilted by Diana Snyder

Assembly Instructions

▷ Create the hobo blocks. For this quilt, I used an equal number of Camp Here blocks (page 40) and Here Is the Place blocks (page 92).

▷ Arrange the pieced blocks into sets of four, 1 wide by 4 long (Fig 1.).

▷ Sew the 1 × 4 blocks into rows. The Wall Hanging Quilt has 2 rows of 6 1 × 4 blocks; the Lap Quilt has 3 rows of 9 1 × 4 blocks; the Twin Quilt has 4 rows of 12 1 × 4 blocks; and the Full Quilt has 4 rows of 14 1 × 4 blocks.

▷ Sew the rows together to complete the inner quilt top.

▷ Quilt. Bind. Enjoy!

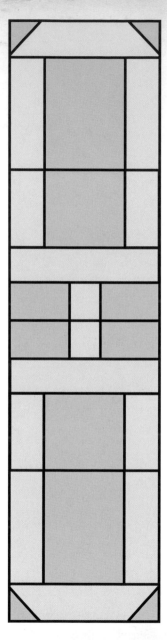

Fig. 1

The Depression days were hard on a lot of people, but at least we had a roof over our heads, our dad had a job, and I think those days taught us a lot about how to get along through the rough times. We survived, and I like to think that some of those gentlemen, those "Knights of the Road," have survived and maybe one of them had something to eat at our back door.

PATRICIA P. SCHREINER,
Michigan

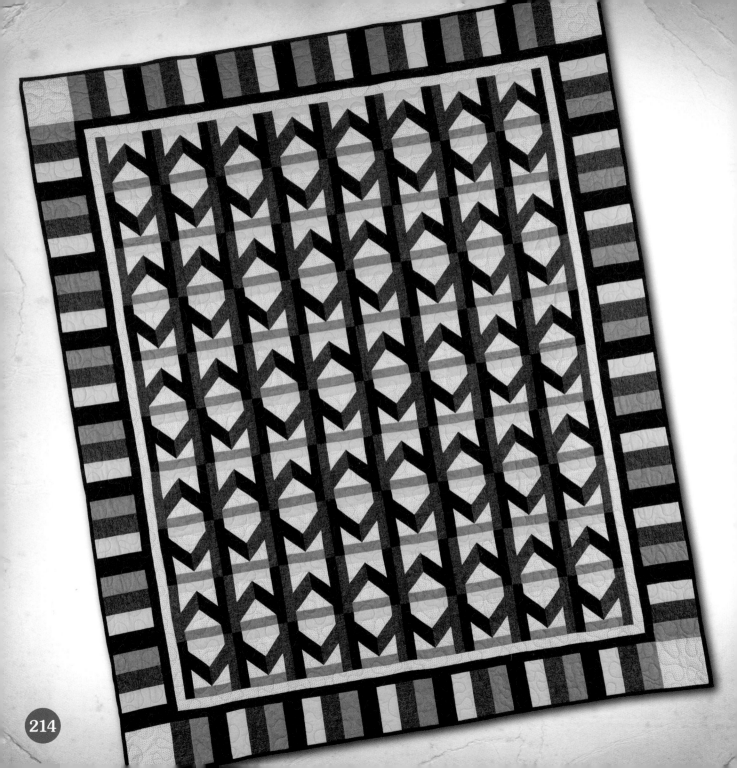

HOBO, TRAMP OR BUM?

The distinction is actually not so easy. Many travelers by freight train were following the crops, working as day laborers. At the time, they were often called "fruit tramps," migrant workers or transients. Some hobos were addicted to alcohol, very much loners and not to be trusted. I guess it's like the adage: I may not be able to define a hobo, but I know one when I see one!

Materials List
for 40" × 52" Throw Quilt

24 Hobo Blocks (Fake Illness, page 74)
Block Background Fabric: ⅜ yard
Dark Blue Block Fabric: ⅜ yard
Light Blue Block Fabric: ⅜ yard
Dark Yellow Block Fabric: ¼ yard
Light Yellow Block Fabric: ¼ yard
Inner Border: ¼ yard
Center Border: ¼ yard
Pieced Outer Border: variety of scraps
Binding: ½ yard
Backing: 2⅔ yards
Batting: 46" × 58"

Materials List
for 64" × 76" Lap Quilt

80 Hobo Blocks (Fake Illness, page 74)
Block Background Fabric: 1 yard
Dark Blue Block Fabric: 1⅛ yards
Light Blue Block Fabric: 1⅛ yards
Dark Yellow Block Fabric: ½ yard
Light Yellow Block Fabric: ½ yard
Inner Border: ⅓ yard
Center Border: ⅓ yard
Pieced Outer Border: variety of scraps
Binding: ⅝ yard
Backing: 4 yards
Batting: 70" × 82"

Materials List
for 70" × 88" Twin Quilt

108 Hobo Blocks (Fake Illness, page 74)
Block Background Fabric: 1⅜ yards
Dark Blue Block Fabric: 1½ yards
Light Blue Block Fabric: 1½ yards
Dark Yellow Block Fabric: ⅝ yard
Light Yellow Block Fabric: ⅝ yard
Inner Border: ⅜ yard
Center Border: ⅜ yard
Pieced Outer Border: variety of scraps
Binding: ¾ yard
Backing: 5¼ yards
Batting: 76" × 94"

Cutting List
for 40" × 52" Throw Quilt

Cut 4 strips 1½" × WOF for Inner Border, then from these strips cut the following:
        2 strips 1½" × 26½"
        2 strips 1½" × 36½"

Cut 4 strips 1½" × WOF for Center Border, then from these strips cut the following:
        2 strips 1½" × 28½"
        2 strips 1½" × 38½"

From Pieced Outer Border scraps, cut the following:
        68 strips 2½" × 6½"
        4 6½" squares

Cutting List
for 64" × 76" Lap Quilt

Cut 6 strips 1½" × WOF for Inner Border, sew together into one strip, then from this strip cut the following:
        2 strips 1½" × 50½"
        2 strips 1½" × 60½"

Cut 6 strips 1½" × WOF for Center Border, sew together into one strip, then from this strip cut the following:
        2 strips 1½" × 52½"
        2 strips 1½" × 62½"

From Pieced Outer Border scraps, cut the following:
        116 strips 2½" × 6½"
        4 6½" squares

Cutting List
for 70" × 88" Twin Quilt

Cut 7 strips 1½" × WOF for Inner Border, sew together into one strip, then from this strip cut the following:
        2 strips 1½" × 56½"
        2 strips 1½" × 72½"

Cut 7 strips 1½" × WOF for Center Border, sew together into one strip, then from this strip cut the following:
        2 strips 1½" × 58½"
        2 strips 1½" × 74½"

From Pieced Outer Border scraps, cut the following:
        134 strips 2½" × 6½"
        4 6½" squares

Designed by Debra Henninger and Debra Greenway, Pieced by Arvella Utley, Quilted by Barb Sidell

Materials List

for 82" × 88" Full Quilt

132 Hobo Blocks (Fake Illness, page 74)
Block Background Fabric: 1⅝ yards
Dark Blue Block Fabric: 1¾ yards
Light Blue Block Fabric: 1¾ yards
Dark Yellow Block Fabric: ¾ yard
Light Yellow Block Fabric: ¾ yard
Inner Border: ⅜ yard
Center Border: ⅜ yard
Pieced Outer Border: variety of scraps
Binding: ¾ yard
Backing: 7⅓ yards
Batting: 88" × 94"

Cutting List

for 82" × 88" Full Quilt

Cut 8 strips 1½" × wof for Inner Border,
sew together into one strip, then from
this strip cut the following:
    2 strips 1½" × 68½"
    2 strips 1½" × 72½"

Cut 8 strips 1½" × wof for Center
Border, sew together into one strip,
then from this strip cut the following:
    2 strips 1½" × 70½"
    2 strips 1½" × 74½"

From Pieced Outer Border scraps, cut
the following:
    146 strips 2½" × 6½"
    4 6½" squares

Materials List

for 88" × 100" Queen Quilt

168 Hobo Blocks (Fake Illness, page 74)
Block Background Fabric: 2 yards
Dark Blue Block Fabric: 2¼ yards
Light Blue Block Fabric: 2¼ yards
Dark Yellow Block Fabric: 1 yard
Light Yellow Block Fabric: 1 yard
Inner Border: ½ yard
Center Border: ½ yard
Pieced Outer Border: variety of scraps
Binding: ¾ yard
Backing: 8¼ yards
Batting: 96" × 106"

Cutting List

for 88" × 100" Queen Quilt

Cut 9 strips 1½" × wof for Inner Border,
sew together into one strip, then from
this strip cut the following:
    2 strips 1½" × 74½"
    2 strips 1½" × 84½"

Cut 9 strips 1½" × wof for Center
Border, sew together into one strip,
then from this strip cut the following:
    2 strips 1½" × 76½"
    2 strips 1½" × 86½"

From Pieced Outer Border scraps, cut
the following:
    164 strips 2½" × 6½"
    4 6½" squares

Assembly Instructions

▷ To create a quilt like the one shown here, use light and dark fabrics to make the Fake Illness block as shown in Fig. 1.

▷ Lay out the quilt top , arranging odd-numbered rows as shown in Fig. 2 and even-numbered rows as shown in Fig. 3.

▷ Sew the blocks together into rows. The Throw Quilt has 6 rows of 4 blocks; the Lap Quilt has 10 rows of 8 blocks; the Twin Quilt has 12 rows of 9 blocks; the Full Quilt has 12 rows of 11 blocks; and the Queen Quilt has 14 rows of 12 blocks.

▷ Sew the rows together to complete the inner top.

▷ Sew the longer inner border strips to the sides of the quilt.

▷ Sew the shorter inner border strips to the top and bottom of the quilt.

▷ Sew the longer center border strips to the sides of the quilt.

 Hobo travels looking for work. A tramp travels but won't work. A bum neither travels nor works. I always considered myself a bit of a Hobo.

GEORGE F. PHILLIPS,
Missouri

▷ Sew the shorter center border strips to the top and bottom of the quilt.

▷ To find the number of 2½" × 6½" strips needed for the pieced outer border strips, calculate as follows: Multiply the number of blocks along a side by 3, then add 2 (for example, if the number of blocks along a side were 10, the calculation would be 10 × 3=30; 30 + 2=32). Sew together the correct number of 2½" × 6 ½" strips for each side of the quilt.

▷ Sew the side pieced outer border strips to each side of the quilt.

▷ Sew the cornerstone squares to each side of the remaining border strips and sew to the top and bottom of the quilt.

▷ Quilt. Bind. Enjoy!

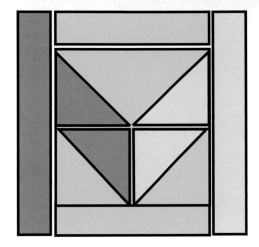

Fig. 1

Fig. 2

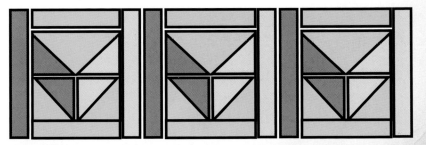

Fig. 3

I had gone to Mack, Colorado to help my brother on an irrigated farm. When the crop was gathered I was headed back to Oklahoma. To save money I caught a freight train and rode it to the coal mines where they switched the empty cars for full cars. I was forced to ride a flat car, and as we got higher in the mountains and into the night hours it started snowing and getting colder by the minute. The snow that stuck to the floor had gotten six or eight inches deep when we started into a long tunnel. The smoke from the engine made me keep getting lower until I was flat on my belly breathing through a crack in the floor. The heat from the engine melted all the snow and was cooking my back.

When we came out of the tunnel and into the blizzard again, the train pulled out on a siding to let another train pass and a breaky made me get into an empty boxcar to keep me from freezing. The only ones in there were a boy and girl, about fifteen or sixteen years old. They were lying on a small pile of sawdust and covered with a thin blanket.

About three in the morning he was trying to get her up but all she would do was cry and beg him to let her lie still.

When he let her lay down she stopped crying instantly. I knew she was freezing to death. I went to them and told him if he didn't get her warmed up she would be dead shortly. I folded the blanket and we rolled her in it so all that was sticking out was her head, arms and feet. Then I put my heavy coat on her with the hood over her head. Then he got on one side and I got on the other. We shook and drug her around until she finally started walking some. We took turns until she stopped crying and started complaining about being cold. We made her run until she was played out. Then we rolled her in the blanket head and foot. He lay down beside her and I emptied my suitcase and piled all my clothes on top of them, then I laid down on the other side.

We slept until the train stopped in Trinidad, Colorado about daylight. I tried to get them to get off and have breakfast with me and warm up but they was afraid of losing their ride. I wished them good luck and we parted. After breakfast I took the highway to Oklahoma.

BILL LAWRENCE,
Oklahoma

Photograph by Rondal Partridge,
Courtesy of the National Archives and Records Administration, 119-cal-5

SIT-DOWN

Many people gave bread, a sandwich or soup to the stranger at their door asking for a bite to eat. But it was a rare event to be invited inside a home and fed at a table.

Materials List
for 35" × 14" Horizontal Table Runner

4 Hobo Blocks
Sashing: ¼ yard
Corner Blocks: ⅛ yard
Inner Border: ⅛ yard
Outer Border: ¼ yard
Binding: ¼ yard
Backing: ½ yard
Batting: 41" × 20"

Cutting List

Cut 3 strips 1½" × WOF for Sashing, then from these strips cut the following:
　　　13 strips 1½" × 6½"

Cut 1 strip 1½" × WOF for Corner Blocks, then from this strip cut the following:
　　　10 squares 1½" × 1½"

Cut 2 strips 1½" × WOF for Inner Border, then from these strips cut the following:
　　　2 strips 1½" × 10½"
　　　2 strips 1½" × 29½"

Cut 3 strips 2½" × WOF for Outer Border, then from these strips cut the following:
　　　2 strips 2½" × 14½"
　　　2 strips 2½" × 31½"

Materials List
for 40" × 12" Vertical Table Runner

5 Hobo Blocks
Sashing: ¼ yard
Border: ¼ yard
Binding: ¼ yard
Backing: ½ yard
Batting: 46" × 18"

Cutting List

Cut 4 strips 1½" × WOF for Sashing, then from these strips cut the following:
　　　2 strips 1½" × 36½"
　　　6 strips 1½" × 6½"

Cut 3 strips 2½" × WOF for Border, then from these strips cut the following:
　　　2 strips 2½" × 12½"
　　　2 strips 2½" × 36½"

Designed by Debra Greenway, Pieced and Appliquéd by Claudette Cremer, Quilted by Jeanette Hammond

Assembly Instructions for Horizonal Table Runner

▷ Arrange the hobo blocks as desired. For this quilt I used the following blocks once each: Free Phone (page 78), Man with a Gun (page 110), Woman (page 144) and Kind-Hearted Lady (page 108). Refer to the photo on page 220 if you'd like to arrange your blocks like the project shown.

▷ Sew a sashing strip to the left side of each block and also to the right side of the last block.

▷ Sew the blocks into a row.

▷ Sew a corner square to the left end of each remaining sashing strip; sew a corner block to the right end of two of the sashing strips.

▷ Sew the sashing strips into two rows.

▷ Sew the long sashing strips to the top and bottom of the runner.

▷ Sew the long inner border strips to the top and bottom of the runner.

▷ Sew the short inner border strips to each end of the table runner.

▷ Sew the long outer border strips to the top and bottom of the runner.

▷ Sew the short outer border strips to each end of the table runner.

▷ Quilt. Bind. Enjoy!

Assembly Instructions for Vertical Table Runner

▷ Arrange the hobo blocks as desired. For this quilt I used the following blocks once each: Talk Religion, Get Food (page 134); Woman (page 144); Sit-Down Feed (page 126); Bread (page 38); and Work Available (page 146). Refer to the photo on page 220 if you'd like to arrange your blocks like the project shown.

▷ Sew a sashing strip to the bottom of each block and also to the top of the top block.

▷ Sew the blocks into a column.

▷ Sew a long sashing strip to each side of the runner.

▷ Sew the long border strips to each side of the runner.

▷ Sew the short border strips to top and bottom of the table runner.

▷ Quilt. Bind. Enjoy!

My experiences made me a lot more humble and I appreciate the smaller things in life—like a good bed and something to eat.

ARCHIE FROST,
Missouri

PHOTOGRAPH BY RUSSELL LEE, COURTESY OF THE LIBRARY OF CONGRESS, LC-DIG-FSA-22076

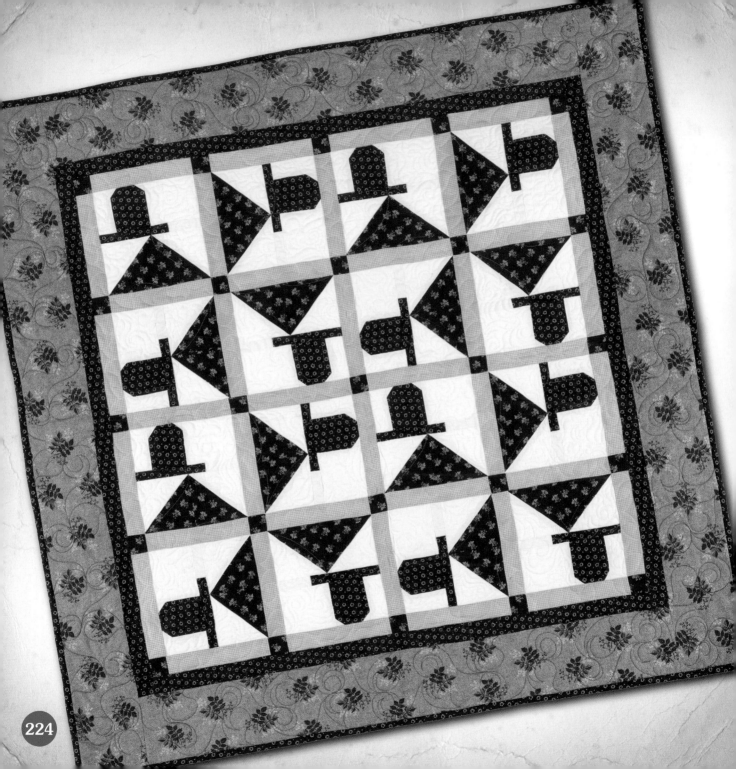

GAY CAT

Many hobos would hide a bit of money in a sock or some other secure spot for an emergency. A Gay Cat was the hobo with enough money hidden away to be able to buy a train ticket if needed.

Materials List
for 39" × 39" Wall Hanging Quilt

16 Hobo Blocks (Rich People, page 122)
White Block Fabric: ½ yard
Red Block Fabric: ¼ yard
Black Block Fabric: ¼ yard
Sashing Strips: ⅜ yard
Sashing Corners: ⅛ yard
Inner Border: ¼ yard
Outer Border: ⅝ yard
Binding: ⅜ yard
Backing: 2½ yards
Batting: 45" × 45"

Cutting List
for 39" × 39" Wall Hanging Quilt

Cut 7 strips 1½" × wof for Sashing Strips, then from these strips cut the following:
    40 strips 1½" × 6½"

Cut 1 strips 1½" × wof for Sashing Corners, then from this strip cut the following:
    25 1½" squares

Cut 4 strips 1½" × wof for Inner Border, then from these strips cut the following:
    2 strips 1½" × 29½"
    2 strips 1½" × 31½"

Cut 4 strips 4½" × wof for Outer Border, then from these strips cut the following:
    2 strips 4½" × 31½"
    2 strips 4½" × 39½"

Materials List
for 53" × 53" Throw Quilt

36 Hobo Blocks (Rich People, page 122)
White Block Fabric: 1⅛ yards
Red Block Fabric: ½ yard
Black Block Fabric: ½ yard
Sashing Strips: ⅝ yard
Sashing Corners: ⅛ yard
Inner Border: ⅜ yard
Outer Border: ⅞ yard
Binding: ⅝ yard
Backing: 3⅓ yards
Batting: 59" × 59"

Cutting List
for 53" × 53" Throw Quilt

Cut 14 strips 1½" × wof for Sashing Strips, then from these strips cut the following:
    84 strips 1½" × 6½"

Cut 2 strips 1½" × wof for Sashing Corners, then from this strip cut the following:
    49 1½" squares

Cut 5 strips 1½" × wof for Inner Border, sew together into one strip, then from this strip cut the following:
    2 strips 1½" × 43½"
    2 strips 1½" × 45½"

Cut 6 strips 4½" × wof for Outer Border, sew together into one strip, then from this strip cut the following:
    2 strips 4½" × 45½"
    2 strips 4½" × 53½"

Materials List
for 53" × 67" Lap Quilt

48 Hobo Blocks (Rich People, page 122)
White Block Fabric: 1⅜ yards
Red Block Fabric: ⅝ yard
Black Block Fabric: ½ yard
Sashing Strips: ⅞ yard
Sashing Corners: ¼ yard
Inner Border: ⅜ yard
Outer Border: 1⅛ yards
Binding: ⅝ yard
Backing: 3⅓ yards
Batting: 59" × 73"

Cutting List
for 53" × 67" Lap Quilt

Cut 19 strips 1½" × wof for Sashing Strips, then from these strips cut the following:
    110 strips 1½" × 6½"

Cut 3 strips 1½" × wof for Sashing Corners, then from this strip cut the following:
    63 1½" squares

Cut 6 strips 1½" × wof for Inner Border, sew together into one strip, then from this strip cut the following:
    2 strips 1½" × 43½"
    2 strips 1½" × 57½"

Cut 7 strips 4½" × wof for Outer Border, sew together into one strip, then from this strip cut the following:
    2 strips 4½" × 53½"
    2 strips 4½" × 59½"

Designed by Debra Henninger, Pieced by Claudette Cremer, Quilted by Sherrie Coppenbarger

Materials List

for 67" × 81" Twin Quilt

80 Hobo Blocks (Rich People, page 122)
White Block Fabric: 2⅛ yards
Red Block Fabric: ⅞ yard
Black Block Fabric: ⅞ yard
Sashing Strips: 1⅜ yards
Sashing Corners: ¼ yard
Inner Border: ½ yard
Outer Border: 1⅜ yards
Binding: ⅝ yard
Backing: 5 yards
Batting: 63" × 87"

Cutting List

for 67" × 81" Twin Quilt

Cut 30 strips 1½" × wof for Sashing Strips, then from these strips cut the following:
> 178 strips 1½" × 6½"

Cut 4 strips 1½" × wof for Sashing Corners, then from this strip cut the following:
> 99 1½" squares

Cut 7 strips 1½" × wof for Inner Border, sew together into one strip, then from this strip cut the following:
> 2 strips 1½" × 59½"
> 2 strips 1½" × 71½"

Cut 8 strips 4½" × wof for Outer Border, sew together into one strip, then from this strip cut the following:
> 2 strips 4½" × 67½"
> 2 strips 4½" × 73½"

Materials List

for 81" × 95" Full Quilt

120 Hobo Blocks (Rich People, page 122)
White Block Fabric: 2⅛ yards
Red Block Fabric: 1⅜ yards
Black Block Fabric: 1¼ yards
Sashing Strips: 2 yards
Sashing Corners: ⅓ yard
Inner Border: ½ yard
Outer Border: 1⅜ yards
Binding: 1 yard
Backing: 7¼ yards
Batting: 87" × 101"

Cutting List

for 81" × 95" Full Quilt

Cut 44 strips 1½" × wof for Sashing Strips, then from these strips cut the following:
> 262 strips 1½" × 6½"

Cut 6 strips 1½" × wof for Sashing Corners, then from this strip cut the following:
> 143 1½" squares

Cut 8 strips 1½" × wof for Inner Border, sew together into one strip, then from this strip cut the following:
> 2 strips 1½" × 73½"
> 2 strips 1½" × 85½"

Cut 9 strips 4½" × wof for Outer Border, sew together into one strip, then from this strip cut the following:
> 2 strips 4½" × 81½"
> 2 strips 4½" × 87½"

Materials List

for 95" × 109" Queen Quilt

168 Hobo Blocks (Rich People, page 122)
White Block Fabric: 4¼ yards
Red Block Fabric: 1⅞ yards
Black Block Fabric: 1⅝ yards
Sashing Strips: 2⅝ yards
Sashing Corners: ⅜ yard
Inner Border: ½ yard
Outer Border: 1⅓ yards
Binding: ⅞ yard
Backing: 8⅝ yards
Batting: 101" × 115"

Cutting List

for 95" × 109" Queen Quilt

Cut 61 strips 1½" × wof for Sashing Strips, then from these strips cut the following:
> 362 strips 1½" × 6½"

Cut 8 strips 1½" × wof for Sashing Corners, then from this strip cut the following:
> 195 1½" squares

Cut 10 strips 1½" × wof for Inner Border, sew together into one strip, then from this strip cut the following:
> 2 strips 1½" × 87½"
> 2 strips 1½" × 99½"

Cut 11 strips 4½" × wof for Outer Border, sew together into one strip, then from this strip cut the following:
> 2 strips 4½" × 95½"
> 2 strips 4½" × 101½"

Assembly Instructions

▷ Lay out the quilt blocks in rows. The Wall Hanging Quilt has 4 rows of 4 blocks; the Throw Quilt has 6 rows of 6 blocks; the Lap Quilt has 8 rows of 6 blocks; the Twin Quilt has 10 rows of 8 blocks; the Full Quilt has 12 rows of 10 blocks; and the Queen Quilt has 14 rows of 12 blocks. Each set of four blocks should form a windmill at the intersection of the blocks (Fig. 1).

▷ Place a vertical sashing strip between each block in every row.

▷ Place horizontal sashing strips and corner blocks between the rows (the sashing strips will be between the blocks and the corner blocks will be at the intersections).

▷ Sew the blocks and vertical sashing strips into rows.

▷ Sew the horizontal sashing strips and corner blocks into rows, beginning and ending with corner blocks.

▷ Sew the rows together to complete the inner quilt top.

▷ Sew the appropriate inner border strips to the sides of the quilt.

▷ Sew the appropriate inner border strips to the top and bottom of the quilt.

▷ Sew the appropriate outer border strips to the sides of the quilt.

▷ Sew the appropriate outer border strips to the top and bottom of the quilt.

▷ Quilt. Bind. Enjoy!

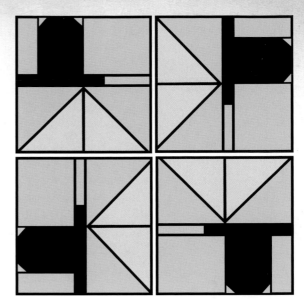

Fig. 1

I was in every state west of the Mississippi before my 18th birthday. Always sent my mother a postcard from every state that I was in, also would find posters, one in Spanish that I sent to my Spanish teacher. It turned out to be an advertisement for a brothel that I hadn't been able to translate before I sent it. She didn't display that one in the classroom, of course.

In 1932 a classmate and I took off from school for New Orleans and the Mardi Gras. A railroad Bull met us there, told us Yankees to get on the highway and up north where we belonged. We waited for a while, thinking he had time to get back to the yard, and started on our way to town. A Ford pick-up stopped, and we were thinking the driver wanted to give us a ride. We were very surprised to see that he was the detective that we just left. He said, "You damn Yankees can't understand plain English, so I will have to learn you a lesson." We were taken to the old "Irish Ditch" jail in the old part of New Orleans where the Justice of the Peace gave us two days in jail because we didn't have $10.00 on us. While in there we were impressed by a high water mark of the 1920s that reached above our heads, and I was 6' at the time. My partner said we had better pray that it wouldn't rain while we were in there. We didn't see any of the Mardi Gras, but we could hear all of the sounds and excitement that was going on. We were released the next morning and advised to get back home and in school. Before we left, we picked up as many beads, paper hats, etc., that we could carry in our shirts. Back at home and in school, we told them that we had been to Mardi Gras and showed them the proof with the things that we had picked up. Later, I confessed to the principal what really happened.

I wouldn't trade all of these experiences for a million dollars; did not get one scratch from any of them. Then, when I worked as a brakeman on the Pennsylvania Railroad in 1952, I lost my left leg just below the knee in an accident at night in the Jeffersonville, Indiana, yards. My lantern saved my life when the conductor on the caboose saw the lantern as the train was leaving. I have lived a productive life since, however. Before this, I was a paratrooper in World War II; before that a professional boxer with a successful career. I have two wonderful sons, wife, five grandchildren, all with college degrees (none wanted to hobo, and I was glad). Now enjoying our six great grandchildren! I have been blessed! I am sure that a lot of prayers were said for my safety. I am sorry thinking how much worry that I must have caused my parents—one regret!

BILLY A. WATKINS,
Indiana

Photograph by Rondal Partridge,
Courtesy of the National Archives and Records Administration, 119-CAL-7

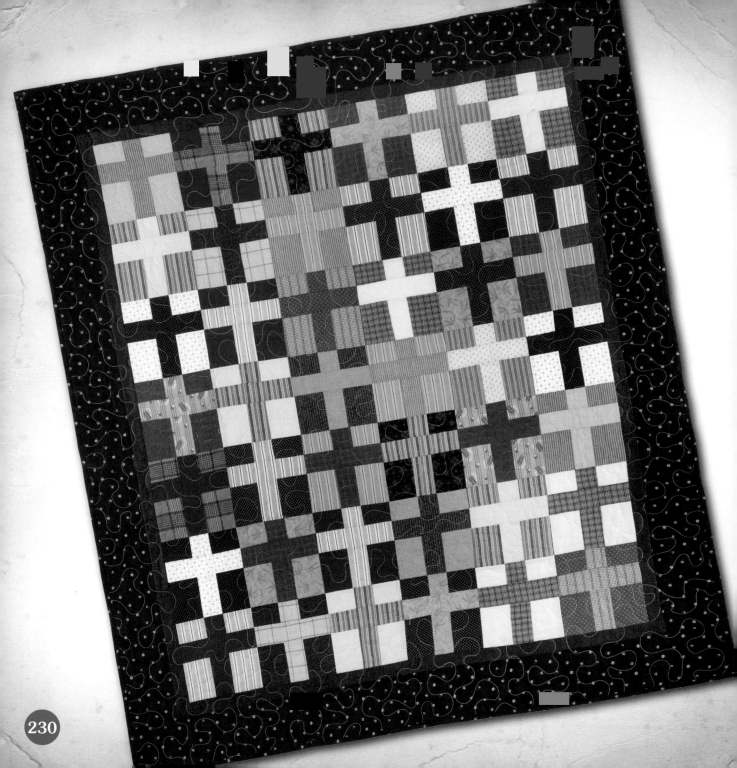

230

CATCH THE WESTBOUND

Most goods were shipped from east to west. As a result there were more empty trains heading east than west, making it easier to travel eastward. To "catch the westbound" meant to die. I don't know if the two facts are related, but it would seem a reasonable assumption to me.

Materials List
for 46" × 52" Crib Quilt

42 Hobo Blocks pieced from scrap fabric (Talk Religion, Get Food page 134)
Inner Border: ¼ yard
Outer Border: ¾ yard
Binding: ½ yard
Backing: 3 yards
Batting: 54" × 60"

Cutting List
for 46" × 52" Crib Quilt

Cut 4 strips 1½" × wof for Inner Border, then from these strips cut the following:
    2 strips 1½" × 38½"
    2 strips 1½" × 42½"

Cut 5 strips 4½" × wof for Outer Border, sew together into one strip, then from this strip cut the following:
    2 strips 4½" × 44½"
    2 strips 4½" × 46½"

Materials List
for 58" × 70" Lap Quilt

80 Hobo Blocks pieced from scrap fabric (Talk Religion, Get Food page 134)
Inner Border: ⅓ yard
Outer Border: 1 yard
Binding: ⅝ yard
Backing: 3⅝ yards
Batting: 64" × 76"

Cutting List
for 58" × 70" Lap Quilt

Cut 6 strips 1½" × wof for Inner Border, sew together into one strip, then from this strip cut the following:
    2 strips 1½" × 50½"
    2 strips 1½" × 60½"

Cut 7 strips 4½" × wof for Outer Border, sew together into one strip, then from this strip cut the following:
    2 strips 4½" × 58½"
    2 strips 4½" × 62½"

Materials List
for 70" × 82" Twin Quilt

120 Hobo Blocks pieced from scrap fabric (Talk Religion, Get Food page 134)
Inner Border: ⅓ yard
Outer Border: 1⅛ yards
Binding: ⅝ yard
Backing: 5 yards
Batting: 76" × 88"

Cutting List
for 70" × 82" Twin Quilt

Cut 7 strips 1½" × wof for Inner Border, sew together into one strip, then from this strip cut the following:
    2 strips 1½" × 62½"
    2 strips 1½" × 72½"

Cut 8 strips 4½" × wof for Outer Border, sew together into one strip, then from this strip cut the following:
    2 strips 4½" × 70½"
    2 strips 4½" × 74½"

DESIGNED BY DEBRA HENNINGER, PIECED BY ALICE BRAMAN, QUILTED BY BARB SIDELL

Materials List

for 82" × 94" Full Quilt

168 Hobo Blocks pieced from scrap fabric (Talk Religion, Get Food page 134)
Inner Border: ⅜ yard
Outer Border: 1¼ yards
Binding: ¾ yard
Backing: 7⅓ yards
Batting: 88" × 100"

Cutting List

for 82" × 94" Full Quilt

Cut 8 strips 1½" × WOF for Inner Border, sew together into one strip, then from this strip cut the following:
- 2 strips 1½" × 74½"
- 2 strips 1½" × 84½"

Cut 9 strips 4½" × WOF for Outer Border, sew together into one strip, then from this strip cut the following:
- 2 strips 4½" × 82½"
- 2 strips 4½" × 86½"

Materials List

for 94" × 106" Queen Quilt

224 Hobo Blocks pieced from scrap fabric (Talk Religion, Get Food page 134)
Inner Border: ½ yard
Outer Border: 1½ yards
Binding: ⅞ yard
Backing: 8½ yards
Batting: 100" × 112"

Cutting List

for 94" × 106" Queen Quilt

Cut 10 strips 1½" × WOF for Inner Border, sew together into one strip, then from this strip cut the following:
- 2 strips 1½" × 86½"
- 2 strips 1½" × 96½"

Cut 11 strips 4½" × WOF for Outer Border, sew together into one strip, then from this strip cut the following:
- 2 strips 4½" × 94½"
- 2 strips 4½" × 98½"

Assembly Instructions

▷ Make the number of blocks needed for the quilt size of your choice. Half of the blocks should have light crosses on dark backgrounds, and half should have dark crosses on light backgrounds.

▷ Arrange the blocks as desired, alternating light and dark blocks. The Crib Quilt has 7 rows of 6 blocks; the Lap Quilt has 10 rows of 8 blocks; the Twin Quilt has 12 rows of 10 blocks; the Full Quilt has 14 rows of 12 blocks; and the Queen Quilt has 16 rows of 14 blocks.

▷ Sew the blocks into rows.

▷ Sew the rows together to complete the inner quilt top.

▷ Sew the long inner border strips to the sides of the quilt.

▷ Sew the short inner border strips to the top and bottom of the quilt.

▷ Sew the long outer border strips to the sides of the quilt.

▷ Sew the short outer border strips to the top and bottom of the quilt.

▷ Quilt. Bind. Enjoy!

PHOTOGRAPH BY RONDAL PARTRIDGE,
COURTESY OF THE NATIONAL ARCHIVES AND RECORDS ADMINISTRATION, 119-CAL-4

One night while waiting for the switchmen to get a train set up, listening to cars being switched from one track to another, and watching the lanterns swinging stop and go signals, we all fell asleep on a side track, unused for a long time with weeds and grass grown high. Perhaps twenty bums had sat or lay there sprawled out. I lay there with my head on the rail, when a vibration awakened me with a start, and in the darkness I saw a lone boxcar that had been switched to this side track, barreling down on us at a terrific speed. I yelled at those around me and dived from the track, as the boxcar thundered by, and believe it or not, everyone made it off the track safely.

DONALD E. NEWHOUSER, *Indiana*

BINDLE STIFFS

A "bindle" was a bedroll. It had one or two blankets, possibly a change of clothes (or at least a dry pair of socks) and any personal items carried by the hobo. It was all rolled up and tied with rope in such a way that a "bindle stiff" could carry it over a shoulder or across the back, making it possible to board a moving train with both hands free.

Materials List

for 55" × 73" Lap Quilt

24 Hobo Blocks of your choice pieced from scrap fabric
Sashing Corners: ½ yard
Light Flying Geese: 1⅛ yards
Dark Flying Geese: 1⅛ yards
Inner Border: ½ yard
Outer Border: 1½ yards
Binding: ⅝ yard
Backing: 3½ yards
Batting: 61" × 79"

Cutting List

for 55" × 73" Lap Quilt

Cut 4 strips 3½" × WOF for Sashing Corners, then from these strips cut the following:
    35 3½" squares

Cut 6 strips 2½" × WOF for Inner Border, sew together into one strip, then from this strip cut the following:
    2 strips 2½" × 43½"
    2 strips 2½" × 57½"

Cut 6 strips 6½" × WOF for Outer Border, sew together into one strip, then from this strip cut the following:
    2 strips 6½" × 55½"
    2 strips 6½" × 61½"

Materials List

for 82" × 91" Full Quilt

56 Hobo Blocks of your choice pieced from scrap fabric
Sashing Corners: ¾ yard
Light Flying Geese: 2¼ yards
Dark Flying Geese: 2¼ yards
Inner Border: ⅝ yard
Outer Border: 1¾ yards
Binding: ¾ yard
Backing: 7⅓ yards
Batting: 88" × 97"

Cutting List

for 82" × 91" Full Quilt

Cut 7 strips 3½" × WOF for Sashing Corners, then from these strips cut the following:
    72 3½" squares

Cut 8 strips 2½" × WOF for Inner Border, sew together into one strip, then from this strip cut the following:
    2 strips 2½" × 70½"
    2 strips 2½" × 75½"

Cut 9 strips 6½" × WOF for Outer Border, sew together into one strip, then from this strip cut the following:
    2 strips 6½" × 79½"
    2 strips 6½" × 82½

Materials List

for 91" × 100" Queen Quilt

72 Hobo Blocks of your choice pieced from scrap fabric
Sashing Corners: 1 yard
Light Flying Geese: 2¾ yards
Dark Flying Geese: 2¾ yards
Inner Border: ⅔ yard
Outer Border: 2¼ yards
Binding: ⅞ yard
Backing: 8 yards
Batting: 97" × 106"

Cutting List

for 91" × 100" Queen Quilt

Cut 9 strips 3½" × WOF for Sashing Corners, then from these strips cut the following:
    90 3½" squares

Cut 9 strips 2½" × WOF for Inner Border, sew together into one strip, then from this strip cut the following:
    2 strips 2½" × 79½"
    2 strips 2½" × 84½"

Cut 10 strips 6½" × WOF for Outer Border, sew together into one strip, then from this strip cut the following:
    2 strips 6½" × 88½"
    2 strips 6½" × 91½"

Designed and Pieced by Debra Henninger, Quilted by Sherrie Coppenbarger

Assembly Instructions

▷ Make the number of blocks needed for the quilt size of your choice. Half of the blocks should use light fabrics and half should use dark fabrics.

▷ Using your favorite method, create 3½" × 6½" flying geese, making the goose from light fabric, and the background from dark. The Lap Quilt requires 54 flying geese; the Full Quilt requires 120 flying geese; and the Queen Quilt requires 153 flying geese.

▷ Lay the quilt top out as shown in Fig. 1. Alternate Row A, Row B and Row C until all rows are laid out. The Lap Quilt has 6 rows of 4 blocks; the Full Quilt has 8 rows of 7 blocks; and the Queen Quilt has 9 rows of 8 blocks.

▷ Sew Row A, then B, then C, and so on until all rows are sewn. Sew the rows together to form the inner quilt top.

▷ Sew the appropriate inner border strips to the sides of the quilt. Some of the top and bottom border strips, depending on the quilt size, are shorter than the side border strips. Measure your quilt top and border strips each time to ensure you are attaching the correct strip.

▷ Sew the appropriate inner border strips to the top and bottom.

▷ Sew the appropriate outer border strips to the sides.

▷ Sew the appropriate outer border strips to the top and bottom.

▷ Quilt. Bind. Enjoy!

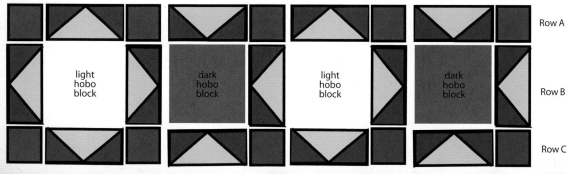

Row A

Row B

Row C

Fig. 1

Don't grieve for me my bosom friend
For I have listened to the wind
Blow down the canyons in the night
And chase the shadows in their flight.
I've rode the rails of the old SP
While the Lord above looked after me.
I've look down from the mountains high
And heard the screaming eagles cry.
I've searched for gold and hunted bear
I think I've been most everywhere.

— ARCHIE FROST,
Missouri

PHOTOGRAPH BY RONDAL PARTRIDGE,
COURTESY OF THE NATIONAL ARCHIVES AND RECORDS ADMINISTRATION, 119-CAL-9

237

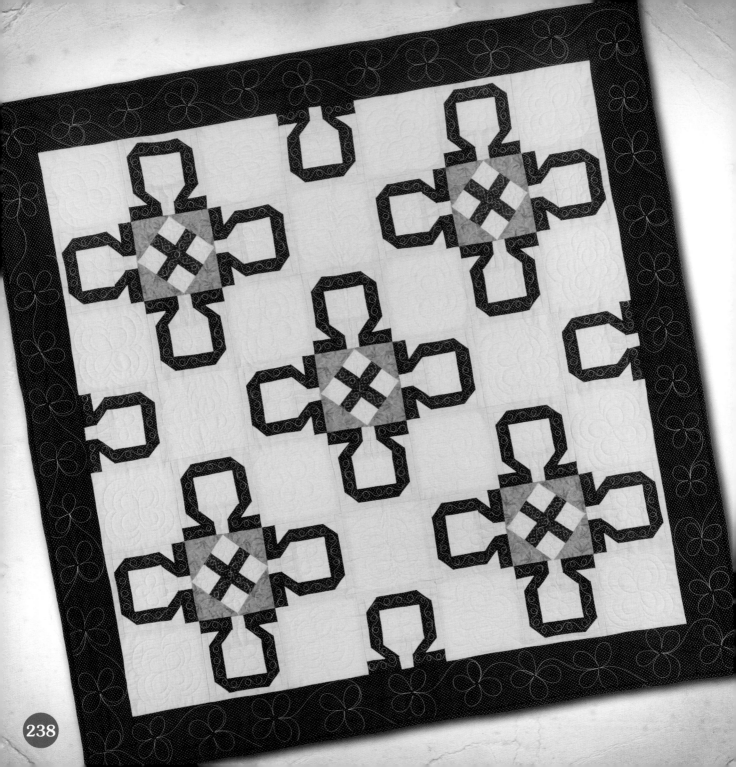

THE BLINDS

The front end of a baggage car, "the blinds," was a very dangerous place to ride. A person could get crushed when the train made a tight curve. The "rods" were the steel bars running below the boxcars, also a dangerous and difficult place to ride. "Riding the blinds" and "riding the rods" were two modes of transportation the more experienced hobos warned against.

Materials List
for 52" × 52" Crib Quilt

49 Hobo Blocks
Background Fabric: 1¾ yards
Yellow Block Fabric: ¼ yard
Green Block Fabric: ¼ yard
Red Block Fabric: ¾ yard
Inner Border: ¼ yard
Outer Border: ⅞ yard
Binding: ½ yard
Backing: 3⅓ yards
Batting: 58" × 58"

Cutting List
for 52" × 52" Crib Quilt

Cut 5 strips 1½" × WOF for Inner Border, sew together into one strip, then from this strip cut the following:
  2 strips 1½" × 42½"
  2 strips 1½" × 44½"

Cut 6 strips 4½" × WOF for Outer Border, sew together into one strip, then from this strip cut the following:
  2 strips 4½" × 44½"
  2 strips 4½" × 52½"

Materials List
for 64" × 76" Lap Quilt

99 Hobo Blocks
Background Fabric: 3¼ yards
Yellow Block Fabric: ⅜ yard
Green Block Fabric: ½ yard
Red Block Fabric: 1⅜ yards
Inner Border: ⅓ yard
Outer Border: 1 yard
Binding: ⅝ yard
Backing: 4 yards
Batting: 70" × 82"

Cutting List
for 64" × 76" Lap Quilt

Cut 7 strips 1½" × WOF for Inner Border, sew together into one strip, then from this strip cut the following:
  2 strips 1½" × 56½"
  2 strips 1½" × 66½"

Cut 7 strips 4½" × WOF for Outer Border, sew together into one strip, then from this strip cut the following:
  2 strips 4½" × 64½"
  2 strips 4½" × 68½"

Materials List
for 64" × 88" Twin Quilt

117 Hobo Blocks
Background Fabric: 3¾ yards
Yellow Block Fabric: ½ yard
Green Block Fabric: ½ yard
Red Block Fabric: 1⅝ yards
Inner Border: ⅜ yard
Outer Border: 1⅛ yards
Binding: ⅝ yard
Backing: 5¼ yards
Batting: 70" × 94"

Cutting List
for 64" × 88" Twin Quilt

Cut 7 strips 1½" × WOF for Inner Border, sew together into one strip, then from this strip cut the following:
  2 strips 1½" × 56½"
  2 strips 1½" × 78½"

Cut 8 strips 4½" × WOF for Outer Border, sew together into one strip, then from this strip cut the following:
  2 strips 4½" × 64½"
  2 strips 4½" × 80½"

DESIGNED BY DEBRA HENNINGER, PIECED BY LILIAN CAGLE, QUILTED BY JERI RENNIE

Materials List
for 76" × 100" Full Quilt

165 Hobo Blocks
Background Fabric: 3¾ yards
Yellow Block Fabric: ½ yard
Green Block Fabric: ½ yard
Red Block Fabric: 1⅝ yards
Inner Border: ⅜ yard
Outer Border: 1⅜ yards
Binding: ¾ yard
Backing: 7 yards
Batting: 82" × 106"

Cutting List
for 76" × 100" Full Quilt

Cut 8 strips 1½" × WOF for Inner Border,
sew together into one strip, then from
this strip cut the following:
     2 strips 1½" × 68½"
     2 strips 1½" × 90½"

Cut 10 strips 4½" × WOF for Outer
Border, sew together into one strip,
then from this strip cut the following:
     2 strips 4½" × 76½"
     2 strips 4½" × 92½"

Materials List
for 88" × 112" Queen Quilt

221 Hobo Blocks
Background Fabric: 3¾ yards
Yellow Block Fabric: ½ yard
Green Block Fabric: ½ yard
Red Block Fabric: 1⅝ yards
Inner Border: ½ yard
Outer Border: 1½ yards
Binding: ⅞ yard
Backing: 8 yards
Batting: 94" × 118"

Cutting List
for 88" × 112" Queen Quilt

Cut 10 strips 1½" × WOF for Inner
Border, sew together into one strip, then
from this strip cut the following:
     2 strips 1½" × 80½"
     2 strips 1½" × 102½"

Cut 11 strips 4½" × WOF for Outer
Border, sew together into one strip,
then from this strip cut the following:
     2 strips 4½" × 88½"
     2 strips 4½" × 104½"

Assembly Instructions

▷ Make the number of hobo blocks required for the size quilt you are making. The Crib Quilt requires 20 blank blocks, 24 No One Home blocks (page 112) and 5 OK blocks (page 116); the Lap Quilt requires 40 blank blocks, 49 No One Home blocks and 10 OK blocks; the Twin Quilt requires 47 blank blocks, 58 No One Home blocks and 12 OK blocks; the Full Quilt requires 65 blank blocks, 82 No One Home blocks and 18 OK blocks; the Queen Quilt requires 87 blank blocks, 110 No One Home blocks and 24 OK blocks. If you'd like to arrange your quilt like the project shown, make the stitch and flip squares of the OK block a different background color (yellow in our sample).

▷ Lay out your quilt as shown in Fig. 1. Be careful that each No One Home block's open end points toward the OK block. Repeat the layout until the correct height and width are achieved: the Crib Quilt has 7 rows of 7 blocks; the Lap Quilt has 11 rows of 9 blocks; the Twin Quilt has 13 rows of 9 blocks; the Full Quilt has 15 rows of 11 blocks; and the Queen Quilt has 17 rows of 13 blocks.

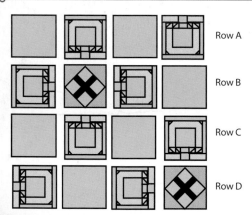

Row A
Row B
Row C
Row D

Fig. 1

▷ Sew the rows together to form the inner quilt top.

▷ Sew the longer inner border strips to each side.

▷ Sew the shorter inner border strips to the top and bottom.

▷ Sew the longer outer border strips to each side.

▷ Sew the shorter outer border strips to the top and bottom.

▷ Quilt. Bind. Enjoy!

Our travels took us then to Belt Junction, six miles out of Indianapolis where our odyssey began. From there we made our way to a relative in Connecticut via Lima, Ohio, to Buffalo, Rochester, and Corning, New York. Here we took an illicit ride on the "Erie Milk Train" bound for Jersey City. It was a harrowing ride between the "blinds" at speeds over eighty miles an hour.

Arthur Huneven,
California

Photograph by Dorothea Lange, Courtesy of the Library of Congress, LC-USZ62-69109

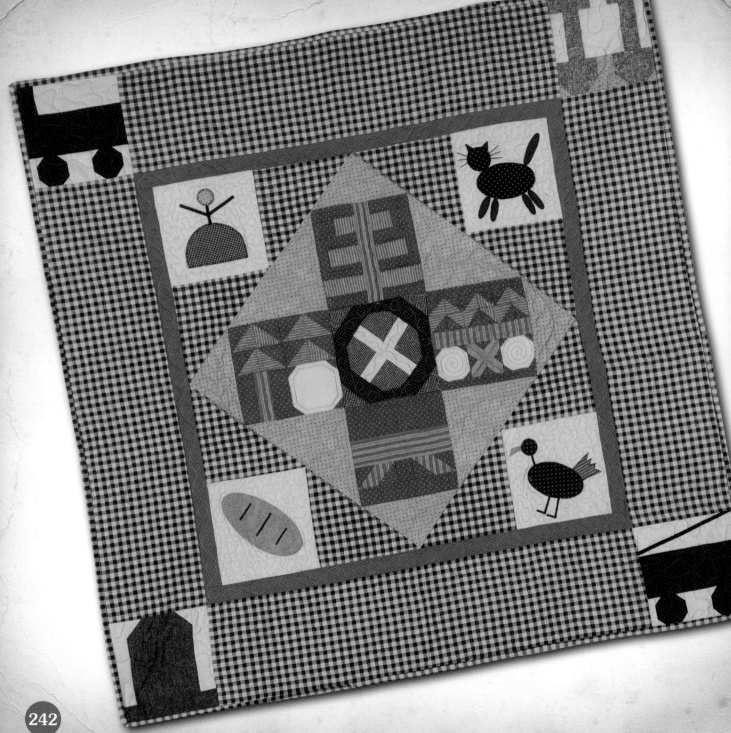

HITCHHIKING

Travel by getting rides in automobiles was a common and accepted mode of transportation. However, getting to one's destination by hitchhiking most often was hit and miss, and painfully slow. Freight trains were faster, easier and more reliable.

Materials List for
38" × 38" Wall Hanging Quilt

13 Hobo Blocks of your choice pieced from scraps
Inner Side Setting Triangles: ⅓ yard
Inner Corner Setting Triangles: ¼ yard
Middle Setting Triangles: ¼ yard
Inner Border: ¼ yard
Outer Border: ⅞ yard
Binding: ⅜ yard
Backing: 2½ yards
Batting: 44" × 44"

Cutting List
38" × 38" Wall Hanging Quilt

Cut 1 9¾ square for Inner Side Setting Triangles, then cut this square in half diagonally twice for 4 quarter-square triangles

Cut 2 5⅛" squares for Inner Corner Setting Triangles, then cut these squares in half diagonally for 4 half-square triangles

Cut 4 6⅞" squares for Middle Setting Triangles, then cut these squares in half diagonally for 8 half-square triangles

Cut 3 strips 1½" × WOF for Inner Border, sew together into one strip, then from this strip cut the following:
  2 strips 1½" × 24½"
  2 strips 1½" × 26½"

Cut 4 strips 6½" × WOF for Outer Border, sew together into one strip, then from this strip cut the following:
  4 strips 6½" × 26½"

{ **HELPFUL HINT** }

This quilt is a great way to use up scraps. You can vary the number of fabrics used in the blocks, but I suggest choosing fabrics in the same tones to pull the blocks together.

DESIGNED BY DEBRA GREENWAY, PIECED AND APPLIQUÉD BY CLAUDETTE CREMER, QUILTED BY JERI RENNIE AND JEANETTE HAMMOND

Assembly Instructions

▷ Arrange the blocks as they will appear in the quilt. For this quilt I used each of the following blocks: Catch out Here (page 42), Work Available (page 146), Woman (page 144), Kind-Hearted Lady (page 108), Officer Lives Here (page 114), Sleep in the Hayloft (page 128), Good Chance for a Handout (page 88), Good Water (page 90), Bread (page 38), Free Phone (page 78), Gentleman (page 80), Catch Trolly Here (page 44), and Sit-Down Feed (page 126).

▷ To create a quilt like the one shown on page 242, sew the Sleep in the Hayloft, Good Chance for a Handout, and Good Water blocks together in a row.

▷ Sew an inner side setting triangle to each side of the Officer Lives Here block, and the Sit-Down Feed block as (Fig. 1).

▷ Sew the Officer Lives Here set to the top of the row of 3 blocks, and the Sit-Down Feed set to the bottom of the row of 3 blocks.

▷ Sew the inner corner setting triangles to this unit to form a diamond. Set aside.

▷ Sew middle setting triangles to adjacent edges of the Woman, Kind-Hearted Lady, Bread and Free Phone blocks (Fig. 2).

▷ Sew each of these corner units to the diamond unit to finish the center.

▷ Sew the shorter inner border strips to each side of the quilt.

▷ Sew the longer inner border strips to the top and bottom of the quilt.

▷ Sew an outer border strip to each side of the quilt.

▷ Sew one of the remaining blocks (refer to the picture on page 242 for placement and direction) to each side of the remaining outer border strips and sew to the top and bottom of the quilt.

▷ Quilt. Bind. Enjoy!

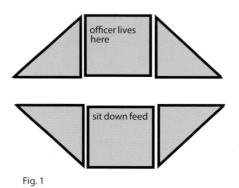

Fig. 1

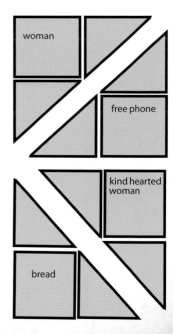

Fig. 2

Floyd and I hitchhiked to Modesto. We got jobs immediately in the fruit. We worked there till the season was over and then hitchhiked to San Diego and got stuck, mind you, on top of the Ridge Route—it was solid mud! This was February, 1934. Then we came back to San Jose, California and worked in the canneries ... We hitchhiked all over the state. We saw California in all its beauty before there were all those superhighways. We saw the glorious fields of hops in Sonora and goats running wild. We had a lovely five years together before we separated ... Floyd remarried and so did I. My husband dies in 1958. I have a lovely son, daughter-in-law and two beautiful grandchildren who don't know their granny rode the rails, and would like to again, but as a guest. I really have something no one can take away from me.

VIOLET PERRY,
Indiana

Photograph by Rondal Partridge,
Courtesy of the National Archives and Records Administration, 119-CAL-10

245

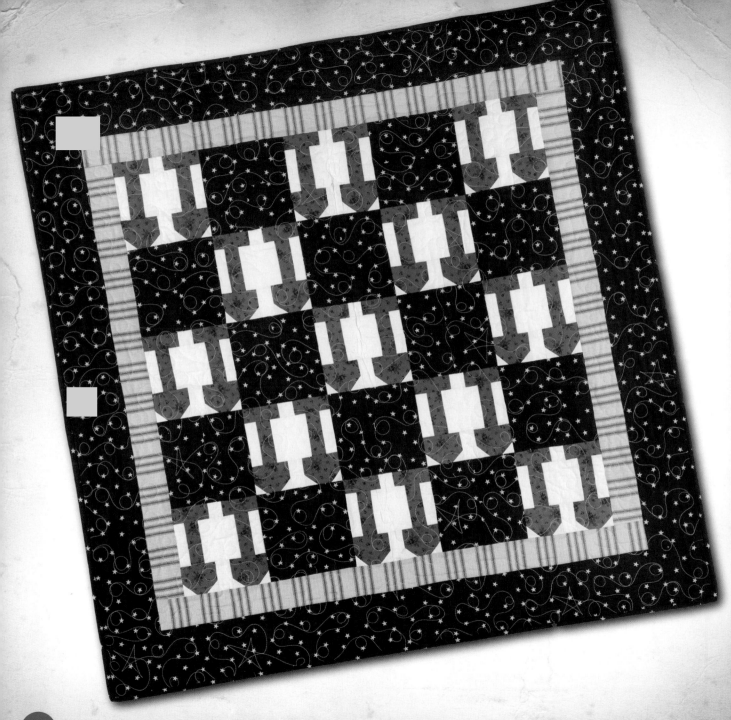

LOOKIN' FOR WORK

There were three basic motives for traveling "free of charge"—as a life style, for an adventure, or in search of work. The overwhelming majority of travelers or hobos were looking for work. Jobs were few and far between. Hard hit, hard-working Americans would go anywhere, any way possible for an honest day's wages.

Materials List
for 42" × 42" Throw Quilt

13 Hobo Blocks (Work Available, page 146)
Dark Block Color: ½ yard
Light Block Color: ⅜ yard
Four Patch Color 1: ⅜ yard
Four Patch Color 2: ⅜ yard
Inner Border: ⅜ yard
Outer Border: ⅞ yard
Binding: ½ yard
Backing: 2¾ yards
Batting: 48" × 48"

Cutting List
for 42" × 42" Throw Quilt

Cut 24 3½" squares from Four Patch Color 1

Cut 24 3½" squares from Four Patch Color 2

Cut 4 strips 2½" × WOF for Inner Border, then from these strips cut the following:
    2 strips 2½" × 30½"
    2 strips 2½" × 34½"

Cut 5 strips 4½" × WOF for Outer Border, then from these strips cut the following:
    2 strips 4½" × 34½"
    2 strips 4½" × 42½"

Materials List
for 60" × 72" Lap Quilt

40 Hobo Blocks (Work Available, page 146)
Dark Block Color: 1⅛ yards
Light Block Color: 1⅛ yards
Four Patch Color 1: ⅞ yard
Four Patch Color 2: ⅞ yard
Inner Border: ¾ yard
Outer Border: 1⅜ yards
Binding: ⅞ yard
Backing: 3⅔ yards
Batting: 66" × 78"

Cutting List
for 60" × 72" Lap Quilt

Cut 80 3½" squares from Four Patch Color 1

Cut 80 3½" squares from Four Patch Color 2

Cut 7 strips 2½" × WOF for Inner Border, sew together into one strip, then from this strip cut the following:
    2 strips 2½" × 52½"
    2 strips 2½" × 60½"

Cut 8 strips 4½" × WOF for Outer Border, sew together into one strip, then from this strip cut the following:
    2 strips 4½" × 60½"
    2 strips 4½" × 64½"

Materials List
for 72" × 84" Twin Quilt

60 Hobo Blocks (Work Available, page 146)
Dark Block Color: 1⅝ yards
Light Block Color: 1⅝ yards
Four Patch Color 1: 1⅓ yards
Four Patch Color 2: 1⅓ yards
Inner Border: ¾ yard
Outer Border: 1⅜ yards
Binding: ⅞ yard
Backing: 5 yards
Batting: 80" × 90"

Cutting List
for 72" × 84" Twin Quilt

Cut 120 3½" squares from Four Patch Color 1

Cut 120 3½" squares from Four Patch Color 2

Cut 7 strips 2½" × WOF for Inner Border, sew together into one strip, then from this strip cut the following:
    2 strips 2½" × 64½"
    2 strips 2½" × 72½"

Cut 8 strips 4½" × WOF for Outer Border, sew together into one strip, then from this strip cut the following:
    2 strips 4½" × 72½"
    2 strips 4½" × 76½"

Designed by Debra Henninger, Pieced by Robyn Welch, Quilted by Suz Tealby

Materials List
for 84" × 96" Full Quilt

84 Hobo Blocks (Work Available, page 146)
Dark Block Color: 2¼ yards
Light Block Color: 2 yards
Four Patch Color 1: 1⅝ yards
Four Patch Color 2: 1⅝ yards
Inner Border: ¾ yard
Outer Border: 1⅜ yards
Binding: 1 yard
Backing: 7½ yards
Batting: 90" × 102"

Cutting List
for 84" × 96" Full Quilt

Cut 168 3½" squares from Four Patch Color 1

Cut 168 3½" squares from Four Patch Color 2

Cut 9 strips 2½" × WOF for Inner Border, sew together into one strip, then from this strip cut the following:
 2 strips 2½" × 76½"
 2 strips 2½" × 84½"

Cut 10 strips 4½" × WOF for Outer Border, sew together into one strip, then from this strip cut the following:
 2 strips 4½" × 84½"
 2 strips 4½" × 88½"

Assembly Instructions

▷ Make the four patch blocks for your chosen quilt size. The Throw Quilt has 12 four patch blocks; the Lap Quilt has 40 four patch blocks; the Twin Quilt has 60 four patch blocks; and the Full Quilt has 84 four patch blocks.

▷ Lay out the blocks, alternating four patch blocks with Work Available blocks.

▷ Sew the blocks into rows.

▷ Sew the rows together to form the inner quilt top.

▷ Sew the shorter inner border strips to each side.

▷ Sew the longer inner border strips to the top and bottom.

▷ Sew the shorter outer border strips to each side.

▷ Sew the longer outer border strips to the top and bottom.

▷ Quilt. Bind. Enjoy!

I will always remember the vast numbers of people riding freight trains in those days. There were entire families going anywhere and everywhere to try and find any kind of work. There were tired and discouraged parents with ragged and hungry kids. The railroad officials made no attempt to keep them off the trains and they filled entire boxcars. They were lined along the track in Oklahoma City for what seemed a half a mile.

Vernon Chadwick,
California

Photograph by Rondal Partridge,
Courtesy of the National Archives and Records Administration, 119-cal-18

SYMBOL GLOSSSARY

A Beating Awaits
You Here

Anything Goes

At the Crossroad,
Go This Way

Bad Dog

Bad Drinking
Water

Bad Tempered Man

Bad Tempered
Owner

Be Afraid

Be Prepared to
Defend Yourself

Bread

Camp Here

Catch out Here

Catch Trolley Here

Chain Gang

Cops Active

Cowards—Will Give
to Get Rid of You

Danger

Dangerous
Drinking Water

Dangerous
Neighborhood

Dishonest Person
Lives Here

Doctor, No Charge

Don't Give Up

Don't Go This Way

Doubtful

Easy Mark

Fake Illness

Food for Work

Free Phone

Gentleman

Go This Way

Good Chance
to Get Money

Good for a
Handout

Good Water

Here is the Place

Hit the Road Fast

Hobos Arrested
on Sight

Hold Your Tongue

Housewife Feeds
for Chores

Jail

Keep Quiet

Kind-Hearted Lady

Man with a Gun

No One Home

Officer Lives Here

OK

Poor Man

Rich People

Road Spoiled—Full
of Hobos

Sit-Down Feed

Sleep in Hayloft

Straight
Ahead

Talk Religion,
Get Food

Tell Pitiful Story

Town Allows Alcohol

Unsafe Area

Well-Guarded House

Woman

Work Available

Worth Robbing

You'll Get Cursed
Out Here

RESOURCES

Photographs courtesy of the Library of Congress can be found on the follow pages: 12, 25, 31, 37, 55, 69, 83, 103, 121, 131, 152, 157, 165, 170, 177, 181, 185, 189, 193, 197, 201, 204, 209, 213, 223, 241

Photographs courtesy of the National Archives and Records Administration can be found on the follow pages: 8, 219, 229, 233, 237, 245, 249

The first-hand accounts included in this book are excerpts from letters from the Uys Family Collection of Teenage Hobo materials, (USM 062), Scottish Rite Masonic Museum and Library d.b.a. National Heritage Museum and are included with the permission of the Scottish Rite Masonic Museum and Library d.b.a. National Heritage Museum. The materials in this collection contain questionnaires, letters, notes from telephone interviews, audiotapes and photographs received by Michael Uys and Lexy Lovell as part of their research in producing the film *Riding the Rails* in 1997. Errol Lincoln Uys then published a companion book to the film by using the primary resources that the co-producers of the documentary film had collected. He published the book *Riding the Rails: Teenagers on the Move During the Great Depression* in 1999. This collection of letters, photographs, and audiotapes where given by several donors. These were Errol Lincoln Uys, Michael Uys and Lexy Lovell. Minor changes have been made to the accounts printed in this book by the author for spelling and grammar.

Recollections from the author's mother, Juanita Penman, which are not a part of the Uys Family Collection, can be found on pages 15, 77 and 197.

Letters from the Uys Family Collection of Teenage Hobo materials, (USM 062), Scottish Rite Masonic Museum and Library d.b.a. National Heritage Museum:

Pages 17, 35, 49, 137 and 228, Billy A. Watkins, Indiana.

Pages 19 and 87, Lyle A. O'Hare, Texas.

Page 21, Charles R. Doty, Oklahoma.

Pages 23–24, Dean Webb, South Dakota.

Pages 27, 33, 54 and 91, James R. Carroll, Pennsylvania.

Pages 29, 39, 109 and 213, Patricia P. Schreiner, Michigan.

Pages 30-31 and 145, Ann Walko, Pennsylvania.

Pages 36–37, 113 and 233, Donald E. Newhouser, Indiana.

Page 41, Michael Corinchock, Pennsylvania.

Page 43, Don Rodgers, California.

Pages 45, 223 and 237, Archie Frost, Missouri.

Pages 47, 85, 97, 105 and 111, Paul Booker, California.

Page 51, Gordon Ayres, California.

Pages 53 and 201, James L. Blackman, Missouri.

Pages 57, 61 and 117, Charles Rankin, Ohio.

Pages 59 and 115, Bud Hughes, Nebraska.

Pages 63 and 193, Malcolm D. Stewart, Indiana.

Page 65, Harriet Dickenson, Indiana.

Pages 67 and 141, Victor Martens, Indiana.

Pages 68 and 18p, Charles N. Bishop, California.

Page 71, Fred Griffin, Missouri.

Page 73, William Csondor, Pennsylvania.

Pages 75 and 157, Ralph H. Shirley, Montana.

Page 79, Ruby LeMunyan, California.

Pages 81 and 123, H.B. "Down the Road Doc" Harmon, California.

Page 82, Roger Brown, Ohio.

Page 89, Frank Kriech, Ohio.

Page 93, Jesse M. Elson, Pennsylvania.

Page 95, Marion Alvin Alley, California.

Pages 99 and 147, Morris M. Thomte, Arizona.

Page 101, Genevieve Woods, California.

Page 102, Ralph Shelly, Ohio.

Pages 107 and 216 George F. Phillips, Missouri.

Pages 119 and 197, Harold Sparks, Virginia.

Page 120, Jo Lamb Fulton, Tennessee.

Page 125, Ben Crump, California.

Pages 127 and 241 Arthur Huneven, California.

Pages 129–130, Edward Rexius, Michigan.

Page 133, Larry Kuebel, Nebraska.

Page 135, Ulan S. Millier, Missouri.

Page 139, Stephen A. Tomko, Pennsylvania.

Page 143, John McKinney, Jr., Nebraska.

Page 149, Betty M. Glover, Virginia.

Page 151, James Pearson, New York.

Page 165, Jack Cash, California.

Page 171, Pat O'Connell, Montana

Page 176, Richard J. Bussell, California.

Pages 181 and 209, William L. Pion, Ohio.

Page 185, Doroty Vorhauer, Virginia.

Pages 204–205, Carl Baird, Michigan.

Page 218, Bill Lawremce, Oklahoma.

Page 245, Violet Perry, Indiana.

Page 249, Vernon Chadwick, California.

INDEX

EVERY QUILT HAS A STORY TO TELL...

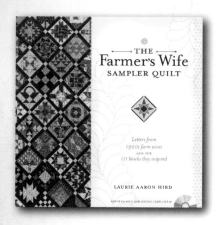

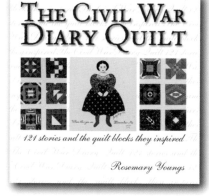

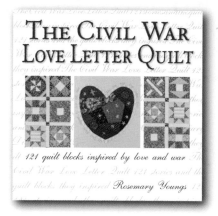

The Farmer's Wife Sampler Quilt
Laurie Aaron Hird

In 1922, *The Farmer's Wife* magazine asked a question: "Would you want your daughter to marry a farmer?" Read excerpts from 42 of the top letters and discover 111 traditional quilt blocks the answers inspired. Each block is fully illustrated and comes with complete cutting templates on the bonus CD.

paperback; 8" × 8"; 256 pages
ISBN-10: 0-89689-828-8
ISBN-13: 978-0-89689-828-8
SRN: Z2991

The Civil War Diary Quilt
Rosemary Youngs

Bring the past alive with distinctive, exquisite quilt blocks that tell the stories of 10 women living and surviving the Civil War. Explore the diary entries of these women, plus instructions for 121 related quilt blocks.

paperback; 8" × 8"; 288 pages
ISBN-10: 0-87349-995-6
ISBN-13: 978-0-87349-995-8
SRN: CWQD

The Civil War Love Letter Quilt
Rosemary Youngs

Get wrapped up in the lives and loves of 11 Civil War soldiers and the beautiful quilt their stories inspired. Using 121 different blocks, you can create any of the 14 projects, including a full-size quilt, lap quilts, wall hangings and table runners.

paperback; 8" × 8"; 288 pages
ISBN-10: 0-89689-487-8
ISBN-13: 978-0-89689-487-7
SRN: Z0751

These and other fine Krause Publications titles are available from your local craft retailer, bookstore or online supplier, or visit our Web site at www.mycraftivitystore.com.